I Think You're Totally Wrong

I Think You're Totally Wrong:

A Quarrel

DAVID SHIELDS AND CALEB POWELL

Alfred A. Knopf, New York 2015

THIS IS A BORZOI BOOK
PUBLISHED BY ALFRED A. KNOPF

Copyright © 2015 by David Shields and Caleb Powell

All rights reserved. Published in the United States by Alfred A. Knopf, a division of Random House LLC, New York, and distributed in Canada by Random House of Canada Limited, Toronto, Penguin Random House companies.

www.aaknopf.com

Knopf, Borzoi Books, and the colophon are registered trademarks of Random House LLC.

Grateful acknowledgment is made to the following for permission to reprint previously published material:

Grove/Atlantic, Inc.: Excerpt from My Dinner with André, copyright © 1981 by Wallace Shawn and André Gregory. Reprinted by permission of Grove/Atlantic, Inc. Any third-party use of this material, outside of this publication, is prohibited.

Revolution Films, Baby Cow Films, and Arbie: Excerpts from The Trip, copyright © 2010. Reprinted by permission of Revolution Films, Baby Cow Films, and Arbie.

Library of Congress Cataloging-in-Publication Data
Shields, David, 1956–
I think you're totally wrong : a quarrel / David Shields and Caleb Powell.—First edition.
pages   cm
ISBN 978-0-385-35194-2 (hardback)—ISBN 978-0-385-35195-9 (eBook)
I. Powell, Caleb.   II. Title.
PS3569.H483413 2015
814'.54—dc23   2014020754

Jacket design by Chip Kidd
Manufactured in the United States of America
First Edition

In the conversation between the authors, certain names and identifying characteristics of persons mentioned have been changed to protect their privacy.

The intellect of man is forced to choose

Perfection of the life, or of the work,

And if it take the second must refuse

A heavenly mansion, raging in the dark.

When all that story's finished, what's the news?

In luck or out the toil has left its mark:

That old perplexity an empty purse,

Or the day's vanity, the night's remorse.

—Yeats

I Think You're Totally Wrong

DAY 1

CALEB POWELL: *(speaking into digital voice recorder)* Current time: 6:30 p.m., Thursday, September 29th, 2011. Place: Seattle. My driveway. David has arrived. I'm going out to meet him.

DAVID SHIELDS: Where do you want me to put my stuff?

CALEB: Back of my car. I'm looking forward to this.

DAVID: Definitely, but did you see the article in the [University of Washington] *Daily*?

CALEB: It's out?

DAVID: *(pulling up the article on his phone)* I must admit I'm a bit flummoxed by your quotes.

CALEB: *(reading the article)* Hmm. I don't see the big deal. She asked me my first impressions of you, and I told her.

DAVID: Do you feel that much animosity toward me, or am I completely imagining it?

CALEB: Animosity?

DAVID: There's hardly a line of yours whose purpose was to do anything but to undermine me.

CALEB: You mean when I said, "Your classes wasted time"? I went on to praise you, but she didn't quote that, of course. And your novel classes did waste time—endlessly dissecting Ted Mooney's *Easy Travel to Other Planets* and Marilynne Robinson's *Housekeeping*.

DAVID: I'd never teach those books now, but still, Caleb—

CALEB: Come in and meet my family.

○

CALEB: *(entering the chaos of the house; the girls swarm at the entrance)* That's Kaya, Ava, Gia.

DAVID: They're adorable.

CALEB: My wife, Terry.

DAVID: Hi, everybody.

CALEB: *(entering living room and speaking first to David, then to his parents, then again to David)* My parents, Dave and Beatrice Powell; David Shields. My parents came to help out with the kids tomorrow.

FATHER: Good to meet you, David.

CALEB: My parents met at Cooper Union.

DAVID: The free-tuition school.

CALEB: *(speaking first to David, then to his parents)* All the paintings in our house are my mother's. David's daughter is a freshman at college in Rhode Island.

DAVID: She goes to RISD.

MOTHER: Risby?

DAVID: The Rhode Island School of Design. RISD.

MOTHER: Never heard of Risby.

FATHER: Your sister Marilyn went there.

MOTHER: Where, Risby?

FATHER: Ris-Dee.

DAVID: It's the Rhode Island School of Design, but they call it RIS-D for short.

MOTHER: Risby?

FATHER: Trice!

CALEB: *(to David)* You wanna beer?

DAVID: I'm good; thanks.

○

TERRY: You're leaving him with your parents?

CALEB: Why not?

TERRY: You're having a beer?

CALEB: One for the road.

TERRY: You excited?

CALEB: I'm ready.

TERRY: What if he makes a move on you?

CALEB: Ha ha.

○

CALEB: *(showing David his shelf of books about Cambodia)* Did you read *The Road of Lost Innocence*?

DAVID: Was I supposed to?

CALEB: It wasn't a coaster. You've had me read, what, fifty books over the last few years, and I give you one?

DAVID: I spent an hour with it, thumbing back and forth. It's not very well written. What's the point? I already know people suffer.

CALEB: It's not trying to be a work of art. Did you get a sense of it at all?

DAVID: It's horrible—what she endured.

CALEB: I'm going to come back to this.

○

CALEB: *(starting the ignition, pulling out the digital voice recorder, placing it on the console)* Current time: 7:07 p.m. You ready?

DAVID: You probably prepared much more assiduously than I did. It'll be an interesting experiment. I'm totally open to it bombing.

CALEB: I want to have a good time.

DAVID: How so?

CALEB: No kids for four days—something to take advantage of.

DAVID: We'll walk, talk, read, cook. I think if we try too hard to have some point-by-point debate, it'll turn out quite stilted. How did you explain this to your parents, your wife? That we're going to go to a cabin for four days to yell at each other, and out of that we'll try to produce a *My Dinner with André*–like exchange? Did that make any sense to them?

CALEB: My dad thinks *My Dinner with André* is about "two homos." I told him it's not.

DAVID: He's homophobic?

CALEB: He's old-school, military, was in Vietnam, but *My Dinner with André* is nothing like us: André talks ninety-five percent of the time as Wally makes quizzical facial expressions.

DAVID: Yeah, but it's an argument about two opposed modes of being. Wally seeks comfort, André seeks discomfort, and they wind up, ever so slightly, changing positions. Same thing in *Although Of Course You End Up Becoming Yourself*. Somehow, when D. F. Wallace slides the tape recorder over to Lipsky's side of the table, the tectonic plates shift. Not sure how. It's beautiful. I definitely want to have an interesting conversation, but the goal, to me, is to come out of this with a book, no?

CALEB: Why don't you commit suicide in the next year?

DAVID: Then we'd have a book for sure. . . . Christ, you were my student—when?—twenty years ago or more.

CALEB: From '88 to '91.

DAVID: And here we are chatting. I wonder what it is about us that gets in the other's grille.

CALEB: Who knows? I never read more than one book by my other ex-teachers, but I've read all yours. I know a lot about you. You know very little about me, so I want to tell my story. I like interviewing people like you, Eula Biss, Ander Monson, Lidia Yuknavitch, Peter Mountford, but I'd much rather converse. When I met Peter, we just agreed, "Fuck it—let's have another beer and finish this up online."

DAVID: Bring in as much of yourself as possible. I want this to be an absolutely equal battle. Let's make it so it's not one-sided, not "Okay, David, tell me what you think about this."

CALEB: Damn straight. Enough about David. You're too academic. Who's lived the more interesting life?

DAVID: I don't accept the premise of the question.

○

CALEB: Terry knows about what we're doing, but not everything.

DAVID: Meaning?

CALEB: You said you wanted homoerotic tension. Were you hitting on me?

DAVID: No. So far as I know, I'm a hundred percent straight. I just thought it might be good subtext to layer in. I'm sure it seems weird—two guys spending four days together in the mountains.

CALEB: You're married, one kid; you wouldn't be the first in that situation with a secret life, fishing, throwing out a few gay-friendly hints. So you say this and I'm thinking, Maybe he's attracted to me, and I'm flattered, but . . . Terry calls this "Date Weekend with David Shields."

DAVID: You don't want her to freak out.

CALEB: That's not the half of it. When she was still in college, she married this guy, Mark, who had his shit together—was in business, loved sports. They divorced after a year. A few months later he came out.

DAVID: Whoa.

CALEB: She doesn't like talking about it. I want to pick at the scabs of experience: mine, hers. She said it was traumatic.

It was relatively early in the era of AIDS. Mark had said he never cheated on her, but she didn't know. She thought she could have AIDS. Mark's dad had even died of AIDS. Her parents are "liberal," but there are grandparents, aunts, uncles. People made a lot of comments. There was a stigma that, no matter how absurd the accusation is, she had made Mark gay. That she'd failed.

DAVID: "If she were sexier, she would have converted him."

CALEB: Mark "married" a Korean guy; they adopted a kid. I've met Mark, and he's sent gifts for our kids. Nice guy. Aside from the basics, though, I've gotten hardly anything from Terry except an offhand detail.

DAVID: Maybe she's waiting to write about it herself.

CALEB: She's not the type, but she's always asking questions, suggesting fantasies, wanting to know if I've ever kissed a man, if I ever wanted to—if I had the opportunity, would I? I'll say, "Only accidentally." When I told her I was going to spend four days with you in Skykomish, she asked, "What would you do if he told you that he could guarantee you getting published, and then he made a move on you?" I said, "You trying to Mark me?"

DAVID: That's a great line in about eleven different ways.

CALEB: I tease back, say that she makes men switch sides.

DAVID: She keeps going to it: sort of, What if? That's fascinating.

CALEB: And there's a short story of mine that relates to all this. I pulled it out of the drawer and reworked it specifically for this trip. You'll see what I mean. Anyway, if you wanted a homoerotic subtext, there's a certain serendipity that you picked me.

DAVID: You can't make this shit up.

CALEB: There are other secrets we'll get to.

DAVID: I like the idea of us being remarkably candid—

CALEB: The thing is—

DAVID: Let me finish. I think of myself—and perhaps I'm kidding myself—but I think of myself as being willing to entertain almost any idea or thought about myself or anything else. I can't imagine me ever saying, "Oh my god, I can't believe you said that." But both of us have to agree about what we can or can't use, don't you think? I might say, "Caleb, we have to leave this in," and you have the right to say no.

○

CALEB: We can't faux-argue like Siskel and Ebert. It's staged, but it can't be fake.

DAVID: Agreed. A genuine disagreement. Civil, but barely.

CALEB: We have real disagreements. You're way too focused on yourself. You're fifty-five. Time to focus on other things.

DAVID: That's why I'm talking to you.

○

DAVID: Any other ground rules? Ideally, our conversation will have an organic flow in which we just fly around from books to women to student-teacher antagonism to that guy you wrote that essay about—Ed Jones?—to whatever.

CALEB: I played ball with Ed the other day.

DAVID: Would he have seen the essay?

CALEB: I don't think so, but one of the guys told me, "I saw that Ed Jones thing you did." I said, "You read it?" And he said, "Every nigga in Seattle's read it. You better hope Ed don't have internet."

DAVID: Where did it appear?

CALEB: The 322 *Review.*

DAVID: I liked it.

CALEB: You seemed to think it was missing something.

DAVID: What I found wanting about the piece—or maybe just the way I'd write it differently—is that I'd question far more than you did your impulse to romanticize him.

CALEB: I didn't romanticize him. I wrote about his domestic violence collar, his divorce, his mooching, being kicked out by his dad.

DAVID: I wanted you to investigate more your liberal white guilt. Make yourself more of the—

CALEB: I don't feel liberal white guilt.

DAVID: Really?

CALEB: Human guilt's another question.

○

DAVID: One of the main ways I've overcome my stutter is that I speak slowly. You have a tendency to cut me off. I've noticed this in other interviews we've done. By all means, I want to give you all the room in the world to talk about anything, but I often get the sense you're not listening to what I'm saying because you're so eager to get in your seven points.

Caleb laughs.

DAVID: You're the poster child for that Fran Lebowitz line: "The opposite of talking isn't listening. The opposite of talking is waiting." I always get the feeling you're just waiting until I'm done so you can talk, and you haven't really engaged with what I've said. I hope I can ask you to listen to what I'm saying. I'll get to my point, and then you go to your point, okay? Is that fair? If we only do these interviews when one of my books comes out, it doesn't really matter, but we're trying to have a real conversation this weekend, and it's important to me that I don't feel incredibly frustrated.

CALEB: Very perceptive on your part.

DAVID: How is that perceptive?

CALEB: My wife observes me interrupting, tuning out what people say, waiting to get my point in. She thinks I'm rude. She read this article on Asperger's symptoms: trouble focusing, trouble paying attention, and so on. She says, "Caleb, that's you—you must have Asperger's." I look at the article and say, "Can't be. I have empathy." She says, "Okay, then you have partial Asperger's, also known as pain-in-the-Assperger's."

Silence.

Hmm. Okay, anyway, with family gatherings, it's not that I have trouble focusing, but that I'm willfully not focusing. I'm paying attention, just not to them. Once, we were sitting around with Terry's parents and sister and Terry, and one of them said, "Caleb, why don't you join us?" And I said, "No thanks, I'm in the midst of internal literary dialogue." With Terry's family I've become "Mr. Internal Literary Dialogue." I just can't focus. I've tried and I can't.

DAVID: Too many micro-discussions of mac-and-cheese?

CALEB: One person talks about what their kids ate last night. The other two or three listen, mouths agape, eyes bulging, waiting to say, "And my son likes peaches but didn't when he was a baby, although he's always liked bananas yakkety-yak-yak."

DAVID: Hey, man, you signed up for stay-at-home-dad duty.

CALEB: I know I come across as pretentious and detached and I'm certain I bore people. My wife thinks I'm arrogant and patronizing, which really isn't—well, isn't always the case. Her family is more successful and less insecure; they're admirable and solid. I can be introverted at family gatherings, even though I'm starving for conversation.

DAVID: I'm by no means the only bookish person you know, but you're eager to flash your chops, show me how I'm wrong.

CALEB: Shit.

DAVID: You miss an exit?

CALEB: A shortcut. We could have saved three to five minutes. It's minor.

○

DAVID: How'd you meet your wife?

CALEB: She's good friends with my sister Sarah, who set us up.

DAVID: And Terry and Sarah are still good friends?

CALEB: Best friends. We all went to high school together, but I hardly said a word to Terry, even though she was friends with Sarah. I didn't talk much to Sarah, either—though Sarah and I are close now. Terry went to the UW [University of Washington] same time I did; she was a poli-sci major and lived with her gay ex-husband a block away from me my last year of school. A year or two after her divorce, she dated a guy twenty years older: the vice president of the Tacoma Rainiers. She stayed with him for four years—his "trophy." She went to sports events, Detlef Schrempf's house in Bellevue, Sonic boxes. At some function she sat by WSU coach Mike Price, and he pinched her ass.

DAVID: Mike Price? Didn't he go to Alabama and get in trouble at a strip club? He said it was a one-time thing.

CALEB: It's never a one-time thing.

DAVID: When did you start dating?

CALEB: 2001. I was between Brazil and Taiwan. We had a long-distance relationship. She came to Asia three times before we got married.

DAVID: You've been married ten years?

CALEB: We got married in 2003. We got married at the same age as you and Laurie, but you're twelve years older. You had Natalie around the same age we had Ava. Natalie's eighteen and Ava's six. Twelve years. This is boring stuff we'll probably take out.

DAVID: It's not boring. We'll just talk, but then when we

talked about your tendency to interrupt, the car got a little cold. You could really feel—

CALEB: Moo!

DAVID: You could really—

CALEB: Moo!

DAVID: There was real tension. Basically, any time we can—

CALEB: Mooooo!

DAVID: We need ninety-seven—

CALEB: Moo! Moo!

DAVID: Okay. I get it. The interrupting cow?

CALEB: "Knock, knock! Who's there? Interrupting Cow. Interrup—Moo!"

DAVID: Did you just come across that?

CALEB: From *Enough About You*. You said that was the funniest joke you ever heard.

DAVID: It was my favorite joke at the time. Seemed like a good thing to say in the Bill Murray chapter, since he's such an interrupting cow.

CALEB: You kept talking and I kept mooing.

DAVID: Noted.

CALEB: I hope you're not one of those types that, you know, never cracks a joke and never acknowledges a joke cracked.

DAVID: I am humor incarnate, my friend.

○

CALEB: What'd you think of *Adderall Diaries*?

DAVID: I don't know. I wanted to love it but didn't. I liked it okay. I like consciousness contending with experience. It felt to me more like experience. What did you think?

CALEB: Murder, sex, drugs, confusion. Good stuff.

○

CALEB: I haven't gotten to Helen Schulman's *This Beautiful Life*. Not sure why you suggested it.

DAVID: It's just an example of the kind of book I think doesn't need to be written anymore.

CALEB: Have you read it?

DAVID: No, but—

CALEB: You're asking me to read books you haven't read?

DAVID: I don't think I said, "Could you read this book?" I just meant, "Caleb, let's bookmark this and talk about it later." I've read a lot about the book, I've read her other novels, and I know her. It's about what happens when a sex tape goes viral at a high school. But we've all already processed this narrative in real time: we already did this novel through the Tyler Clementi case.

CALEB: There was the Billy Lucas suicide and so many others.

DAVID: That was DeLillo's big idea twenty-five years ago: terrorists are the new novelists.

CALEB: You probably didn't read *We Need to Talk About Kevin*, then, either.

DAVID: Really great title, but what novel could ever touch Columbine?

CALEB: A friend of mine wrote a novel about a pop-star celebrity—how he picked up boys and took them to his mansion, etc. His agent wouldn't even send it out.

DAVID: Why not?

CALEB: The main character was transparently Michael Jackson. The topic was too controversial, I guess.

DAVID: For a long time I wanted to write about Tonya Harding. These moments really grip you during the time they're happening, but I've come to realize that for me, anyway—

CALEB: *(stops car)* Uh-oh.

David looks intently out the windshield.

CALEB: Jeez, I wasn't even going fast. I saw the crosswalk but didn't see her. I'll wait until she crosses.

○

CALEB: *How Literature Saved My Life*—the title doesn't work.

DAVID: Seriously?

CALEB: *How Literature Saved* Your *Life*?

DAVID: The good thing about it is that it doesn't need a subtitle. "What's it about?" Well, it's about how literature saved my life.

CALEB: That's every book you write. Didn't Steve Almond already write *How Rock 'n' Roll Saved My Life*?

DAVID: *Rock and Roll Will Save Your Life.* Did you see that thing Almond and I did? Someone interviewed me, then she asked Almond to criticize my answers. It was supposed to be funny.

CALEB: He seems like a cool guy.

DAVID: He's lively.

CALEB: His persona, when he's in his element, works. He should be a comedian, but he's not a serious writer— "serious" being a writer who writes about "serious" topics.

DAVID: In person he's charming. And he's quick, insanely quick. I like him, even if I'm not a huge fan of his work, and I think the feeling is mutual. I find his stuff a little superficial, don't you?

CALEB: He hasn't earned the right to be a political authority. Not that I have, either, but I'm not going around issuing self-indulgent moral stands that have no substantive value. Sartre refused the Nobel Prize. How many lives did that save? Almond was teaching at Boston College—

DAVID: Where he quit.

CALEB: —when Condoleezza Rice was invited to give the commencement speech.

DAVID: You wonder if there wasn't another motivation on his part.

CALEB: It got him on Fox News.

DAVID: I saw something by him recently called "Twenty Tough Questions for Barack Obama." A very, very stock liberal critique of Obama. I come close to sharing virtually all of Almond's politics, but I don't pretend to be a political scientist. He always winds up writing 1,500-word articles for *Slate* called "Steve Almond's Solution to the Palestinian Crisis."

○

DAVID: Did you ever feel compelled to have a conventional profession?

CALEB: No.

DAVID: Did you actively seek out a bohemian life?

CALEB: After college I worked construction and tried to be a musician. I never considered a career or saving for the future.

DAVID: How did you tend to support yourself abroad?

CALEB: Teaching ESL: English as—

DAVID: I know what "ESL" stands for. Did Terry ever put any pressure on you to have a career?

CALEB: No. She's pretty good about it. It's not like I'm a doctor and could walk into a six-figure job. And taking care of the children is a job. I could see myself teaching later.

DAVID: Do you have genuine expertise as an ESL teacher?

CALEB: No.

○

DAVID: In any case, the point being, I wonder if we've married slightly more rational and commonsensical people than we are ourselves. You wife is in advertising?

CALEB: Close enough. Technically, sales, but linked to marketing/advertising. And your wife's at Fred Hutchinson—fund-raising?

DAVID: She's a project manager. They study things like whether night-shift workers are more likely to get prostate cancer. Did you ever go out with people in the arts?

Writers? Does it surprise you that you married someone who's not an artist?

CALEB: Yeah.

DAVID: Me, too.

CALEB: When I was overseas, I never thought I'd marry an American. I thought I'd settle overseas. Probably Asia.

DAVID: Then, in 2003—

CALEB: Sorry to interrupt . . .

DAVID: No, go ahead.

CALEB: How much of your stuff does Laurie read? Does she criticize drafts? Does she read only the published book? Does she like your work?

DAVID: I'd say it's one of the sadnesses of my life. She reads my work and she semi-likes it sometimes—there'll be passages she likes—but she's not exactly riveted. She liked *The Thing About Life* okay, I think, and she liked *Dead Languages*, but that was a long time ago. She's a huge David Foster Wallace fan; she's always apotheosizing Wallace. Enough about Wallace!

She's a very smart person who's not literary, so she'll say, "I read *Reality Hunger*, and I kind of agree with it. I, too, am weary of fiction." And that will be her whole comment. It's a book I spent years writing, but it's not in her to say, "It's brilliant," or on the other hand, "I liked this, but I quarreled with that." In general, she's not crazy about my work. How about Terry? Has she read all your essays and stories?

CALEB: No. You remember my story set in Thailand—the one I gave you, published in *Post Road*? Terry still hasn't read that story. It's four pages. I told her I'd like her to read it, showed it to her, put it on her nightstand, and left it there. If she's read it, she never told me. The only things she likes come from my *Notes of a Sexist Stay-at-Home Father* family blog. I write stuff like "What do you call a guy who hates giving women backrubs?"

DAVID: Is this a joke?

CALEB: A massage-ynist. But my serious stuff she hates or isn't interested in. I have to twist her arm to read any of it. She usually finds it boring, calls me a "literary snob."

DAVID: And yet she mocks your preference for beer over wine.

CALEB: She loves Harlan Coben. He writes the Myron Bolitar series. She'll say, "You'd like Myron Bolitar because he was a basketball player, number one draft pick for the Celtics who blew his knee out and became an agent who cleans up athletes' messes. Not only that, it's verrrrrrrrrrrrrry literary!" Two months ago, when you and I marked this trip on the calendar, I said to her, "Give *Reality Hunger* a shot. I'm really interested in your take; it'll give us something to talk about. I'm going to leave this book on the night table, and please take a look." She said, "Okay." She still hasn't read it.

DAVID: And you put it there in August?

CALEB: Yes.

DAVID: Laurie is capable of the same.

CALEB: But she likes Wallace.

DAVID: That's not generally her taste. Maybe it's a Midwestern thing. "Shipping Out," "The Illinois State Fair," "Consider the Lobster," and "Host," but those are it. Non-writers could never fathom the hurt inflicted—or maybe they can.

CALEB: My dad read that *Gulf Coast* Q&A you and I did and called it literary fluff. Sarah read our interview in the *Rumpus* and couldn't get past the fact that we said "fuck" a few times. I didn't know what to say. Then Sarah read a few pages of *Reality Hunger* and wasn't impressed, and Terry shares Sarah's opinion, even though she hasn't read a word of it.

DAVID: Some galleys of *How Literature Saved My Life* arrived while I was away. Natalie said, "We opened the box not knowing what it was, and then we read it. We really liked it. So funny!" I asked, "How far did you get?" They stopped at page twenty. There's a heavy-duty sex scene at about page fifty that I'm glad they didn't get to, but I was just sort of baffled that they'd read and stop after twenty pages. Not even curious? I wonder if it has something to do with not wanting to know about that part of you.

CALEB: Terry hates the way I analyze everything. I pushed some books on her that she liked: Rian Malan's *My Traitor's Heart,* Jung Chang's *Wild Swans,* Maugham. Then she wanted me to read *Water for Elephants* and *Stones from the River.* I'm open, but I immediately started dissecting. She says I don't like books because of envy, because I'm unpublished. As if, all of a sudden, I'm going to like these books as soon as I'm published.

DAVID: Would Terry read *Thing About Life*?

CALEB: She'd probably like that more than *Reality Hunger.*

DAVID: Maybe she'd like *Dead Languages.*

CALEB: She might.

DAVID: She wants smooth entertainment. What does she like beyond Simón Bolívar or whatever his name is?

CALEB: Oprah selections: Rohinton Mistry. Amy Tan. Lisa See.

DAVID: Those are probably not terrible.

CALEB: She's a big David Sedaris fan. She's always, "Why can't you be funny and write like David Sedaris?"

◠

DAVID: Did Terry ever read your rape novel?

CALEB: Maybe ten percent. She says she supports my writing, and if I ever get published, she expects me to write in the acknowledgments, "I thank my wife for her loving support." She supports me as a father and husband but not as a writer. She endures my writing. My passion could be race car driving or eating hot dogs for all she cares. I don't know if she'll even read this.

DAVID: Sounds like she wouldn't.

CALEB: Well, I'm not going to edit myself. I realize family or intimates don't like to see themselves portrayed in an uncomplimentary manner. Writers turn to fiction to protest, perhaps.

DAVID: You're still invested in fiction in ways that I'm not.

◠

CALEB: *(to the DVR)* September 29th, 2011, 8:38 p.m. Caleb and David are departing from the parking lot at Red Apple Market, in Sultan, Washington, where they bought groceries. Groceries and beer.

DAVID: So who's this guy whose house we're staying at?

CALEB: Khamta. He's with his wife and son in Hawaii. His wife is his ex-girlfriend's ex-girlfriend.

DAVID: Yowza.

CALEB: His wife and ex are/were bi.

DAVID: Got it. How do you know him?

CALEB: I grew up in Coupeville—fifty miles north of Seattle. Two friends from high school, Dave Barouh and Khamta Khongsavanh, built houses outside of Skykomish. I worked on both houses. Barouh's is smaller and the power has a problem, so we'll probably stay at Khamta's.

DAVID: I'm happy to stay wherever you want. What are my requirements? Warm. I like heat. And I'd like to take some walks.

CALEB: I have a Washington State Parks pass. We can do casual or serious hikes. I know the terrain. Whenever I'd work on these houses, I'd stay a few days. Terry calls them work vacations.

DAVID: Is it hard to leave? Are the girls fine being with Terry?

CALEB: They favor her. When she comes home, they leave me and pounce on her. My wife's a better wage earner, and if she were a full-time mom, she'd be better at that, too.

DAVID: I'll bet you're better at it than most men would be.

CALEB: I'll give myself that.

○

DAVID: What's the state of your novel? I thought it was emi-
nently publishable (whatever that means). Didn't Sarah
Crichton at FSG [the publisher Farrar, Straus & Giroux] like
it a lot?

CALEB: She was hooked by the beginning but thought it lost
momentum.

DAVID: That would have been so great.

CALEB: Would have been. You liked my novel but didn't
love it.

DAVID: I think that's fair.

CALEB: I had to push you to read it.

DAVID: I'm a hard sell: I'm not interested anymore in the conventional novel.

CALEB: My novel's been rejected by some really great editors.
My agent tried her best, got it to the right people.

DAVID: Where's she based?

CALEB: D.C. Her biggest clients are a congresswoman named
Barbara Lee and Helen Thomas until she dumped Helen
after her anti-Semitic tirade. She didn't change a word of my
manuscript, just sent it off. She sells genre fiction and nonfiction by politicians and journalists. I'm the only "literary"
writer she has. It's time for me to switch.

DAVID: It's best not to tell an agent or an editor what's going
on until you have to. You have to be willing to piss people
off.

CALEB: That shouldn't be a problem.

○

CALEB: We just passed Baring. One grocery store/post office. Same building. We're near Stevens Pass.

(parking in front of a run-down house)

What do you think?

(long silence)

DAVID: Okay.

CALEB: Let's go in.

DAVID: Okay.

CALEB: We've got different senses of humor.

DAVID: I find stuff funny. I just don't laugh all the time.

CALEB: Look at that house. You'd stay there?

DAVID: Why not?

CALEB: I wondered whether to do this. I told my wife, and she said, "Really?" You'd have a stoic expression, and I'd tell you that it was a joke, and you'd say, "Huh?"

DAVID: You should do it, whatever it is. Ah, I see. I'm an idiot. You were going to pretend this horrible place is where we were staying, and I would freak out.

CALEB: Pretend?

DAVID: If you're joking, it would be the kind of thing I'd laugh at.

CALEB: This house hasn't been lived in for ten years. No lights, grass four feet high, broken windows. I was working up to telling you we're staying at a meth lab. Sensors, wires, and pit bulls. You'd stay here?

DAVID: I could handle it.

CALEB: *(driving farther on the dirt road)* I give up.

○

CALEB: Skykomish, September 29th, 2011, 8:57 p.m. We're about one mile south of Highway 2 and three miles west of the town of Skykomish. We turned off Money Creek Road, down a dirt road, a driveway, and are entering Barouh's house.

DAVID: This is nice.

CALEB: He should rent it out. The ghost of Barouh is all around. I just wanted to check the gas stove. If the gas doesn't work, we'll go to Khamta's.

○

CALEB: Khamta's house.

DAVID: This isn't our place, is it?

CALEB: Outdoor basketball court, kids' wading pool, hot tub. He's got four-wheelers and a riding mower. It's no cabin.

DAVID: Christ, it's gorgeous. I'm going to send a picture of it to Laurie.

○

CALEB: *(playing a CD inside the house)* You're friends with the singer.

DAVID: Is it Rick Moody's band?

CALEB: Mountain Con.

DAVID: Oh my god! James sounds great. Wow! Man! They sound terrific. It's so cool that you looked him up.

CALEB: I didn't. I saw him perform about eight years ago and bought the CD. When you mentioned Mountain Con in that essay, I looked at my CD and noticed James Nugent's name.

DAVID: They sound great. It's so polished. What's the name of the song?

CALEB: "Future Burn Out." You didn't recognize it? You've written about them.

DAVID: I must admit I didn't. I have the ear of a penguin.

CALEB: You ready for some music and chess?

○

CALEB: There's a cold war going on: art vs. life. Shields vs. Powell.

DAVID: Man, I can barely remember.

CALEB: Are you that rusty?

DAVID: I'll give it a shot.

CALEB: Ain't like riding a bicycle.

DAVID: I'll try. If I get killed, so be it. This is the queen *(thump)*. Queen on color.

CALEB: She has a necklace. These pieces *are* odd looking. It's the chess set my dad had as a boy. The king has a beard.

DAVID: I'll start and go out with a bang.

. . .

DAVID: *(thump)* I like the idea of a little chess game where I get mad. It'd be hard to transcribe. I'm playing a little recklessly. What was my mistake? Shoot. Dumb. What am I thinking?

CALEB: *(laughing)* That's staying in.

DAVID: Like Wallace when he loses at Ping-Pong. Hmm. My mistake. What an idiot. Oh my god.

CALEB: You haven't played chess in a while.

DAVID: Helpless. You're good, but this is all pretty basic stuff. I'm oblivious. Boy, I was just excited that some of the moves came back to me. This one's over.

. . .

CALEB: *(setting up the pieces)* I can't play chess at home, on the road, or around Terry.

DAVID: Why not?

CALEB: If I play, I tune out and she goes bananas. I never play chess on my computer.

DAVID: Why not?

They begin another game.

CALEB: Same as why I stopped smoking pot. I wouldn't be able to stop. On our honeymoon, she and I were in Flores, Guatemala, and stopped off at an internet café. Terry finished her email and I told her that I wanted to finish my chess game, so she went to our hotel, about a five-minute walk away. An hour later—she'd say three hours—she comes back and I'm still playing chess.

DAVID: Computer chess?

CALEB: Yahoo Games.

DAVID: Have you gotten good?

CALEB: My game has stayed more or less the same as it was in high school. A friend and I play through email. One game lasts weeks. Anyway, from the first game I could see that you haven't played in a while. You made an unorthodox opening.

DAVID: I played seriously the year I had a broken leg in high school. The apex of my chess career was dreaming in chess notation.

CALEB: Want another beer?

DAVID: No thanks. *(thump, thump, thump)* Let's see, I move there, you grab this guy . . . *(thump)* I get confused sometimes.

○

CALEB: I'd like to teach my daughters chess. Chess helps you think. You can make a lot of analogies to life. Most people think intuitively. Chess exposes this. Namely, what looks good at first glance, prima facie, might be an error. And from that you learn to question judgment. Speed chess, on the other hand, is more instinctual.

DAVID: Obviously.

CALEB: "Look before you leap" or "see a chance—take it." What do you do? Okay, you have two objects: one is worth a dollar more than the other, and they are worth a dollar ten total. How much is each object worth?

DAVID: Unless I'm missing something, isn't one object a dollar and the other a dime?

CALEB: That's a difference of ninety. One's worth a hundred and five. The other's worth five.

DAVID: True that.

CALEB: You have doors A, B, and C. Behind two of the doors are goats and behind one is a car. You pick door A. The announcer goes to door B and opens it: it's a goat. He asks you if you want to take door C or keep door A. Should you switch doors?

DAVID: The guy could be lying, so what difference does it make?

CALEB: Assume he's not. Three doors: behind two are goats, and behind one's a car. Whatever door you pick, you get what's behind.

DAVID: And you want a car?

CALEB: No, you live in the Himalayas and want a goat. When you pick door A, he opens door B and there's a goat, and he hasn't opened door A or C yet, but he gives you the option of switching from A to C. Do you switch?

DAVID: I gotcha.

CALEB: Do you switch?

DAVID: To door C? Umm, I would say no. I'd stay.

CALEB: Wrong. If you switch, you'll have a two-in-three chance of getting the car. If you stay, you have a one-in-three chance.

DAVID: Isn't there still, at this point, an equal one-in-two chance?

CALEB: No. You switch and you always have a two-in-three chance of getting the car.

DAVID: Is that really true?

CALEB: By switching, you can expatiate your wrongness two out of three times.

DAVID: I'm not sure "expatiate" is the right word.

CALEB: You have to switch.

DAVID: Are these math puzzles?

CALEB: Math and logic.

DAVID: Are you good at math?

CALEB: I scored two hundred points higher in math than verbal on the SAT. I was an average English student.

DAVID: I barely passed trigonometry. Hearing all these logic puzzles makes me think about something a student told me the other day about David Wagoner. Did you ever study poetry with him?

CALEB: No.

DAVID: Perfect example of misapplied logic.

CALEB: Hold that thought. I've got to pee.

◐

DAVID: When Wagoner taught, he required his students to present their work by reading it aloud in class. That way he wouldn't have to read their work on his own time.

When Wagoner retired ten years ago or so, David Guterson got up and told a funny story about how whenever he tried to track down Wagoner for a response to his work, Wagoner would say, "Just keep writing." Guterson pretended that Wagoner was actually providing deep Buddhistic wisdom, forcing the apprentice back onto his own resources. Wagoner stalked out of the ceremony, furious.

The story this student told me was that Wagoner advised his grad students, "Don't smoke. Don't drink. Don't do drugs. Don't have too many sexual partners. Be a cautious, risk-averse person because—look at me—I'm eighty-four, I still have this mane of silver hair, and I'm still cogent and writing poems and you, too, if you're lucky, at eighty-four, can—"

CALEB: I saw this blog once that posted a list of keys to being a writer and one was not drinking.

DAVID: That's such an inadequate response to existence, and Wagoner's work suffers from exactly the same caution: every poem he writes is about how he took a walk in the woods and came across a snake or a dying ember, which turns out to be a symbol of something or other. I know I'm guilty at times of being overly careful about health and food, etc., but even I know the point of life can't be to die at ninety-two safe and secure in your jammies.

○

CALEB: This girl, a friend from Whidbey Island, Samantha, had a fling with Harv—his name is Harvey, but we call him Harv. It's a good story and happened here in Sky when Harv was staying out here. And before I begin I'd like to say that that writing mantra "show—don't tell" is bullshit.

You don't show stories; you tell them. Too many writers "show."

DAVID: No kidding. I'm the one who taught you that twenty years ago.

CALEB: Write expediently. Speak expediently. Okay, Samantha and Harv were colliding into each other. Backstory: Ten years earlier, Harv had a fling with Jen while Jen had a boyfriend. Six months later Harv bumps into Jen at a party and she's six months pregnant. Harv says, "Mine?" Jen says, "It's not yours." A year goes by and Jen calls. "Harv, my boyfriend made me give the baby a paternity test. It's not his. Come on in." So Harv goes in and boom, he's a dad. Ten years later Harv and Jen are together, and then Samantha comes into the picture.

At the time Samantha was seeing Jefferson, a meth head ex-con. Jefferson and Samantha dated for four years. Anyway, when Jefferson was five, he saw his seven-year-old sister hit by a car. They lived in a trailer park and the local drunk nailed her. Jefferson went home and told his mom. His sister died. Later, Jefferson married young, at twenty-two, and has a two-year-old son. Son contracts a disease, they perform tests on Jefferson, and Jefferson discovers he's not the biological father.

DAVID: At this time is Jefferson with Samantha?

CALEB: No, this is years before Samantha. Like I said, it's backstory. Jefferson confronted his wife, she confesses— big blowup and breakup. Since then Jefferson learned a trade, he works, but when things get bad he turns to drugs. He's nice, quiet, introverted, and not an idiot. He once was reading *Moby-Dick*. I tried to talk to him about it. "What do you think?" And he gave one-word answers. "Good." Or: "Interesting." He's fifteen years older than Samantha. Samantha's young, cute, and fun. We don't know why Samantha keeps going back to him. She wants out. It just drags on and on.

So when Harv and Samantha hook up, they carry unhappiness. Harv tells Samantha he and Jen are kaput, invites Samantha to Skykomish. Samantha and Harv spend a couple days here, everything's great, and then Jen calls and says she's driving to Skykomish with their ten-year-old son. Evidently, Harv and Jen are not kaput. Jen's an hour away. Harv is trying to get Samantha out the door. Six weeks later Samantha finds out she's pregnant.

DAVID: Have these people not heard of birth control?

CALEB: Go figure. Samantha's sweating for a few days. It turns out the fetus is Jefferson's. Samantha dumped Jefferson and now has a four-year-old son. Jen left Harv, got a degree from the UW, and now works at Boeing. Harv's derailed but hanging on. Same with Jefferson.

DAVID: You've got a good bad novel on your hands. I don't really have anything to say other than "There it is: real life comin' at ya."

CALEB: What sort of response is that?

DAVID: There's no particular larger—

CALEB: It's just what happened. It's not a—

DAVID: Do you know the Danish TV show *The Killing*?

CALEB: My sister lived in Denmark for four years. When she was here this summer, she dropped off the whole series. My parents are watching it now.

DAVID: Twenty one-hour episodes. It's not great, but it's

good. You watch it in Danish with huge English subtitles. By the end, you've convinced yourself you know Danish. It's an endlessly elaborated investigation into the murder of a high school girl. . . . This song is so beautiful.

CALEB: "Jesus Don't Want Me for a Sunbeam."

DAVID: That voice, the bottomless sadness of that voice. . . . I get bored easily by the plot, it takes a million times too long to get there, but it finally builds to something very beautiful. Brag points: I figured out who the killer is in the first episode. It—

CALEB: Aargh. Stop. Anyone who didn't appear in episode one will be eliminated as a suspect.

DAVID: Uh, it actually wasn't in the first episode, come to think of it. It felt like the first episode. I figured it out toward the beginning. The killer may have been anywhere in the first several episodes. Anyway, what these twenty episodes build to is this: the men are always certain, and they always get it wrong. Basically, men know nothing and women know everything, intuitively. In some sense it's a feminist parable disguised as a detective story, but it's very delicately done. The merest bass line thrumming away. When you told your story about Jen cheating on her boyfriend and then Harv cheating on Jen and then Jefferson seeing his sister die and becoming a meth head and on and on, I was only slightly interested in it. It was just a "story." It has to flip over into something, into "X." I need an X factor. Without that, it's just life.

○

CALEB: Let's talk about that former student of yours you keep writing about—the guy who served time in prison for "shooting a dude" and whose prison credo "Do your own time" you don't like.

DAVID: "His stoicism bores me."

CALEB: Why keep writing about him?

DAVID: I'm running out of ideas. That's where you come in. You're fresh blood.

CALEB: Ha ha.

DAVID: I'm serious.

CALEB: I want to know more about this guy. Did he kill or injure his victim? Was it assault? Was it murder? Manslaughter? How many years did he serve? In your books, the only question you ever ask is, "How do we deal with the fact of mortality?" In essence, "We die. What do we do about that?" That's your modus operandi, but I'm interested in why we kill.

DAVID: Why people commit individual murders or genocide?

CALEB: In Vollmann's *Butterfly Stories* there's a restaurant owner in Phnom Penh who survived the Khmer Rouge, watched them kill his wife and children, and did nothing because if he'd showed emotion, he, too, would have been killed. Vollmann writes a sentence or two about suffering and moves on. I wanted Vollmann to stay.

DAVID: And what I loved is that Vollmann moved on. He knew we could fill in the blanks. That's where the art comes in.

CALEB: I grew up around Cambodia, metaphorically. My parents went to Angkor Wat in 1956; they shot 16mm film. My dad was in Saigon for a year, and he has a lot of books from that era. They subscribed to *National Geographic*. I remember this issue: "Kampuchea Wakens from a Nightmare." I was maybe twelve years old. After college, Cambodia became an obsession. I became engaged to a Cambodian woman; it lasted a year. Later, I went to Cambodia. I'm now writing a Cambodian woman's biography. That's my X factor: suffering, the sociopath, the serial killer, atrocity, Pinochet, Pol Pot, Idi Amin, what motivates Ted Bundy?

DAVID: Do you somehow think that will get you closer to anything?

CALEB: It seems futile, but yes, I do.

DAVID: Yeah, let's hear about another murder. You got the happy solution to murder?

CALEB: What's frustrating is the vacuum. No one's interested in Cambodia, but we follow celebrity waistlines. Books about Cambodia and such: I read these books over and over again.

DAVID: What kind of books—genocide porn?

CALEB: Atrocity can become cliché, but—

DAVID: I'm much more interested in pulling back and seeing the big picture.

CALEB: Huh?

DAVID: My closest friend, Michael, has been spending the last decade writing a book called *Investigation into the Death of Logan*. His father died in Vietnam in '63, almost certainly a suicide. His wife, Norma, died at forty-six of cancer. And German soldiers in World War II had to return home from the Eastern Front because the war had made them insane. Michael is convinced that he and Norma decided she didn't need to get a biopsy—when she did—because Michael had been so obsessed with his father's death for so long that the two of them, Norma and Michael, just couldn't deal with any more incoming. What Michael loves about the German soldiers is that they couldn't handle the war. Through them, Michael—

CALEB: There's no satisfying X factor to life: people suffer and die, and that's it, but that's what I'm interested in. Let's get to life, not this evasion of life, not "escaping reality" hunger. Maybe your friend thinks he's gotten to something, but it's personal and not universal.

DAVID: I couldn't disagree more. You're missing the entire point of art.

CALEB: I get what life's about.

○

DAVID: Sometime soon I want to write a book where I talk to three guys around the corner from me: the owner of a French bakery who fled from Vietnam, an Iraqi guy who runs a mailing service, and the owner of the overpriced restaurant Kabul, who left Afghanistan.

CALEB: That's a book I'd read.

DAVID: I'm sure I cartoonize you, too, but I think you cartoonize me as unaware of the world. I think of myself as political.

CALEB: Politically naive.

DAVID: Let me get to my point. I'm also interested in why

human beings behave the way they do—how could I not be? You're trying to take the position of "Open it up—I want to hear about people's lives." Okay. Sometimes, though, my reaction is just "Heard it. Heard it. Tell me something new." The endless complications of that soap opera you were spinning out—this guy fucked that girl and that girl fucked this guy—who gives a shit? I don't know these people. You know them; they're part of your life. Me, I'm bored. You have to cut to the fucking chase: what's the point?

CALEB: That's a legitimate response. You investigate abstract questions; you keep circling back to them. You want these serious epistemological and existential questions: What's "true"? What's knowledge? What's memory? What's self? What's other? What's death? I'll quote Gertrude Stein: "There ain't no answer. . . . That's the answer." I want to ask questions that have substantive answers: Why do we kill? Why do we inflict pain? Why do we suffer? How can we stop suffering?

DAVID: And I'd say the only way you can get at those questions seriously is to watch how you yourself think.

○

DAVID: A former student of mine is writing about her marriage to a Libyan Muslim. She's a blonde beauty from San Diego. Her daughters wear the veil. She and her family live in the Research Triangle in North Carolina. Her name's Krista Bremer.

CALEB: Is she Christian?

DAVID: Not particularly.

CALEB: In name only?

DAVID: I guess.

CALEB: Because it's illegal if she's not "of the book"—namely, a Jew or a Christian.

DAVID: But don't be atheist.

CALEB: Or Hindu or Buddhist or Wiccan. When I worked in the United Arab Emirates I had to fill out paperwork, and my employers told me to check the "Christian" box, even if I wasn't. Also, and I realize you're more Jewish than me—

DAVID: I'm not really that Jewish.

CALEB: You were raised that way. In that one story, your stand-in uses an anti-Semitic slur, tells his father, and the father goes ape. I never had that.

DAVID: You're Jewish?

CALEB: Yeah.

DAVID: You are?

CALEB: Persian. My grandfather was born in Iran, though my father was born in Lebanon. He's Sephardic.

DAVID: That's a major surprise. Not that it particularly matters, but with a name like Caleb Powell—

CALEB: My father's name, at birth, was David Jamil Mizrahi. He came to America when he was two.

DAVID: Hold the back page, as my father used to say.

CALEB: My grandfather, his dad, Jamil Mizrahi, died when my dad was five. His mother was named Powalski and changed it to Powell. As a single woman in the 1940s, she had to fight her in-laws for custody and compromised by keeping my dad in Jewish school. Then she remarried a

Catholic when my dad was nine. I'm just a quarter Jewish. Supposedly I can become an Israeli citizen based on this.

DAVID: Do you think of yourself as Jewish in any way?

CALEB: Not religiously. Ethnically, a little.

DAVID: Culturally, does it resonate?

CALEB: I'm fascinated by it. Whenever I bring it up, Terry will say, "Oh, you just want to be Jewish." Yeah, like I want to be black, too.

DAVID: "Caleb": it's such a religiously loaded name.

CALEB: Moses sent twelve spies to Jerusalem and only Joshua and Caleb did God's work. Joshua got an entire book. Caleb got a few lines. My father went to Jewish school, then Catholic school, and came out neither. I suppose he considers himself Christian. He says, "I know it's silly, but I believe in God." We rarely talk about it.

○

CALEB: You ever believe in God?

DAVID: Zero. How about you?

CALEB: Yeah.

DAVID: Really? Surely not now.

CALEB: You read my novel twenty years ago. I don't expect you to remember. It's partly about a Christian youth who loses faith.

DAVID: I didn't know how autobiographical it was. What was the title again?

CALEB: *This Seething Ocean, That Damned Eagle.*

DAVID: I'm obsessed with titles, and no offense, Caleb, but that has got to be among the worst titles I've ever heard.

CALEB: That's what you said twenty years ago, too.

○

CALEB: I never became serious about life until I was twenty-six or -seven. Until then I focused on art, writing, and music. Then I switched and focused on life. And the best artists focus on both.

DAVID: Writing a book is as much an experience as falling in love.

CALEB: If you're a writer, you can't focus only on life as depicted through art. Externally, you have to live, then internally create your art.

DAVID: It doesn't work like that. It's the Yeats line: perfection of the life or perfection of the work, but not both. You've got to choose. It's the only way to get anything done. Most people live through life. Not that many people live through art.

CALEB: You've worked hard. You've written a lot of books.

DAVID: People always praise me for "working hard," but it's the only thing I can do. You've immersed yourself in life much more fully than I have. You probably wish you'd written books that had been published. Whereas my portico gates slammed down a long time ago. It's obviously a concern of mine: by focusing so much on art, have I closed myself off so completely from—

CALEB: Yeah: the stutter, masturbation, acne, basketball heroics, the girlfriend whose diaries you read, the journalist parents who always did the "right" thing. I can't objectively evaluate your writing because I know you, but at times it's like you're writing one long book.

DAVID: It's true of everyone. Everyone has only one—

CALEB: Could you go a month without writing, but live extreme?

DAVID: I'm sure I have.

CALEB: Stupid question.

DAVID: No, it's an interesting question. I'm always working on a book. It's pathological. The moment I'm finishing one book, I absolutely have to, as if I were an addict, create a windstorm around a new project.

○

CALEB: Ken Kesey stopped writing because he said he wanted to live a novel rather than write a novel.

DAVID: Such bullshit.

CALEB: It's partly a copout, but he has a point. I wanted to be a writer in college. I wrote one novel, kept rewriting it in your class, and then I said I wanted to live a novel before writing one. It's not like I completely stopped, but writing took a backseat. I've written four books, along with stories and essays that could make another, but from the age of twenty-three to thirty-five I stopped writing creatively.

Writing was always the goal of experience—traveling to forty countries, learning several foreign languages, spending eight years overseas. I kept a journal in the UAE and you could count that as a book. If I didn't write, I compensated by reading. I read compulsively.

DAVID: How old are you now?

CALEB: Forty-three.

DAVID: So what is your larger point?

CALEB: Just that I think you're partly right: writing is so hard, you can't compromise. Sometimes I wish I'd chosen art. I submit to a lit mag and a grad student editor half my age tells me I'm backing into sentences with too many subjunctive clauses.

○

DAVID: You remind me at times of my college friend Azzan, who was born in Israel, grew up in Queens. Big man on campus: walked around with a khaki-colored, military-looking jacket and a purposeful stride. Compared to the other intellectuals at Brown, he seemed so assured. A ladies' man, a year or two older. I admired him, even idolized him to a degree. He always said he was going to become a writer. He spent junior year abroad, had a torrid affair in Paris. Got a Rhodes scholarship and at Oxford focused mainly on boxing. He went here, went there, was always saying, "Oh, I'm just gathering material for my great novel.

You can't write without living your life." I've always thought it was his mistake, substituting experience for writing, but maybe it's my mistake. Maybe he didn't really want to be a writer in the first place. He's nearly sixty now and now he's ready to write, but it's too late for him to become a serious writer.

CALEB: What are you trying to say?

DAVID: Your writing is interesting, and getting more so, but—

CALEB: It could be better.

DAVID: It's stuff you should have been doing twenty years ago.

○

DAVID: *The Trip* was originally six half-hour episodes on BBC, which later got edited down into a two-hour movie. I much prefer the show, but this is the movie—hope you like it.

Steve Coogan: Hey, Rob, Steve. . . . Are you free? . . .
Rob Brydon: Why me?
Steve: Well Mischa is unavailable. You've met Mischa, haven't you? . . . I've asked other people, but they're all too busy. So, you know, do you wanna come? . . . There's a small fee, which I'll split with you, sixty–forty.

. . .

Rob: It's 2010. Everything's been done before. All you can do is do something someone's done before but do it better or differently.
Steve: To some extent, that's correct.

DAVID: To some extent, that's incorrect. If I believed that, I'd slit my wrists.

CALEB: I agree. Nothing is exactly the same. Every work of art is both original and influenced by other works. You want this flip at the end, like at the end of Wallace and Lipsky, but maybe I come out of this more convinced that I'm right and you're wrong.

DAVID: Hmm. Not sure we self-consciously say that we're trying to do all that, do we? Is that gonna work?

Magda the Hotel Clerk: Sorry, we only have one double room for you. . . .

Rob: We can share, that's all right.

Steve: No we can't. . . .

Rob: This is a huge bed. We could easily share this bed.

Steve: It might be huge to you. . . .

Rob: What's the problem, anyway? What do you think's gonna happen?

. . .

Mischa: (on phone with Coogan) You think I'm gonna go to Las Vegas and become a prostitute?

. . .

Rob: (to his wife, Sally, on phone) Could I interest you in some rather salacious . . . I'm not wearing any pajama bottoms . . .

. . .

Rob: Don't you find it exhausting, still running around going to parties and chasing girls at your age?

Steve: I don't run around and go to parties. I don't run around and chase girls.

Rob: You do . . .

. . .

Steve: Do you find it exhausting looking after a baby?

Rob: Yes . . .

. . .

Man on Street: Are you Steve Coogan?

Steve: Yes, I am.

Man: Aha!

Steve: Aha.

Man: All right, man. How you doing?

Steve: Fine, thanks. . . .

Man: Can I ask you a question?

Steve: Yeah, of course, absolutely.

Man: Is it true what I read about you?

Steve: What do you read about me?

Man: That you're a bit of a cunt.

Steve: Well, where did you read that?

Man: It's in today's newspaper. Here, look. (Holds up a newspaper with the headline "COOGAN IS A CUNT")

Steve: Uh, whoever said that doesn't know me very well.

Man: Are you sure? (Unfolds newspaper with full headline: "COOGAN IS A CUNT SAYS DAD")

. . .

Steve: I'm sure people think we're gay.

Rob: I don't care.

. . .

Rob: (at home after the trip) Hello . . .
Sally: I've missed you.

. . .

Steve walks around his empty apartment, looks through his mail,
sighs. Piano music.

. . .

Rob: (playing with his daughter, then sharing dinner with Sally) . . .
delightful homecomings . . .

. . .

Steve: (watching a video of himself with Mischa, then leaving a
message on his agent's voice mail) I'm not going to do the HBO
pilot . . . I've got kids . . . Bye.

. . .

Rob: (hugging Sally) I don't like being away from you.

. . .

Steve is alone in his apartment.

. . .

Film ends. Credits.

DAVID: It's pretty great, isn't it? We're watching the trading
of skins. I love that moment when Brydon, even though he

thinks of himself as a domestic man, comes on to that girl and gets rebuffed.

CALEB: You almost want to see what would have happened.

DAVID: The way he crawls back to his original position on the couch—it's hard to watch.

CALEB: He's relieved he doesn't have to go through with it. Did he do it because he's not happily married?

DAVID: To me, no. It's because he feels pressure from Coogan to act out. Then, of course, at the end, there's Coogan, looking forlornly at his copy of *Vanity Fair.*

CALEB: "I'm not going to do the HBO pilot. I've got kids. Bye."

DAVID: It's incredibly beautiful, but the first time I watched it I thought (and Laurie did, too) the ending was a little too easy. I wish they hadn't oversold the pathos.

CALEB: It's almost a happy ending, even a moral ending, which I thought you were supposedly against.

DAVID: I cry at *Friday Night Lights.*

CALEB: Coogan chooses fatherhood. And Brydon probably feels relieved he didn't cheat, as he returns to his wife and child.

DAVID: I can feel Coogan's loneliness at the end. It's quite palpable.

CALEB: And he realizes this. Even though his children live with his ex, he chooses them. He won't advance his career if it means he'll be a nonexistent father.

DAVID: I think I'm starting to fade. I'll see you tomorrow, Caleb.

CALEB: Good night.

DAY 2

CALEB: Did you and Laurie ever discuss having a second kid?

DAVID: Yes. In what was probably not my greatest moment, I said no.

CALEB: No?

DAVID: I was teaching twelve months a year—four quarters at the UW plus any visiting teaching gigs that came up—to make ends meet, and had no time to write. Now all I do is think about Natalie, but those first couple of years I wasn't hugely loving being a parent, I must admit. And, probably most importantly, Laurie and I weren't getting along that well.

CALEB: What's the age difference between you and Laurie?

DAVID: We're the same age. She had the famously bad formulation of "We're not getting along that great, so let's have a second kid." My response was "I'm pretty ambivalent about almost everything, but one thing I'm certain about is that I don't want a second child. I'm sorry." I wasn't draconian. I just said, "That's the way I feel. How do you feel?" And she said, more or less, "I'm not a hundred percent certain, and if you're pretty certain, I'll yield to that." That's my memory; I should ask her if I'm remembering correctly. I do remember talking about it with her later, and she said, "If I had really wanted to have had another child, I would have just had one," which at the time I remember thinking was the most amazing thing I'd ever heard. Men are apparently that manipulable. I know the conventional wisdom is that if one person, especially the woman, wants a second child, you're supposed to say, "Aye aye, Cap'n." I didn't do that. It was a very selfish decision, mostly having to do with writing and a little having to do with not wanting to be paying college tuition when I was sixty-five. My feeling at the time was "Let's raise Natalie and we'll see where we are then, and if we wind up getting divorced, each of us'll still be fifty-four. Not dead yet." Pretty pathetic.

CALEB: Did you say that to her?

DAVID: No, but I remember Laurie saying at one point that if we didn't have Natalie to connect us, she didn't know why we would stay married. For a variety of reasons that I can go into if you want, I now feel very happily married, and I couldn't imagine not being with Laurie, but like any marriage, our marriage has had its ups and downs, and that was undoubtedly its—

CALEB: Nadir.

DAVID: And it wasn't horrible; it was just one discussion. It's one of Laurie's best traits: she moves on. At least to me, she presents as the queen of non-regret. But if we had never had a child, the marriage would almost certainly have ended.

CALEB: That's something you decide before you get married. Didn't you talk about how many kids you wanted?

DAVID: No.

CALEB: How many years were you together before you got married?

DAVID: Four years.

CALEB: And it never came up?

DAVID: Both of us were equally ambivalent. When it came up, we just said, "We'll see." I'm very "female" in wanting to talk about everything, but Laurie never wanted to talk about it. You guys had specifically agreed: three children?

CALEB: We talked beforehand: as many as three, no more. The first two turned out well, so what the heck, we tried for a third. Terry wanted only girls. If we had a fourth, she'd want another daughter.

DAVID: Wait—what's wrong with the male sex?

CALEB: She's great with her mother. They talk daily. Her mom was only nineteen when she conceived Terry. She's like an older sister. Both Terry's parents are cool—quasi hippies or ex-hippies, although I don't think that's how they see themselves now.

DAVID: How old are your kids?

CALEB: Six, five, and two. Terry was, respectively, thirty-five, thirty-six, and thirty-nine when she had them. She's a year younger.

DAVID: Why three? Why not two or four?

CALEB: We each are the oldest of three siblings. I'd been living in Asia up until we got married, and when we got married we immediately tried for a child. Terry was thirty-four, we didn't want to wait, and she got pregnant almost instantly. We married in June and by September she had her twelve-week checkup. We lived in a condo. I worked construction, and I played basketball at Green Lake almost every day. I wanted to get into this basketball culture now that I was back in Seattle: make friends, be cool.

All summer I asked guys if they wanted to have a beer with me after playing. After an hour or two of ball, I could blow a twenty on a round or two of beers and then go home. I put my neck out. Terry would ask me about my day. And I'd tell her, "Oh, I took Darryl or Tyrone or James or Sniper to the Green Lake Tavern for a couple of beers." And she'd say, "Who paid?" I'd say, "It was my invite." She'd say, "They ever invite you? They're taking advantage of you, aren't they?" I'd tell her I didn't care, and that I was new. If you invite, you pick up the check.

Terry's pregnant, and she has her three-month appointment. I'm playing basketball, and Tyrone asks me if I'm up for a beer. First time I get an invite. Hell yeah. It felt cool. We're on court, winding down, and all of a sudden I see Terry on the sideline.

DAVID: And she's pregnant?

CALEB: This is the first time she's ever watched me play. Game ends, I go to the sideline, and she says, "I miscarried."

DAVID: Oh my god.

CALEB: Tears and hugs. We go have a cup of coffee near Green Lake, and I tell her we'll try again. She tells me we have to wait at least six weeks. They have to perform this procedure to remove the remnants of the fetus. On the way back, in the parking lot, there's Tyrone, and he's like, "What's up? We gonna have that beer?" I look at Terry, and she says, "I'll meet you at home. You do what you want."

DAVID: Did Tyrone know your wife had miscarried?

CALEB: Not yet. Terry has gone to her car, and I'm thinking, well, I feel like a beer, and what more can I say? I've done my duty. So I go with Tyrone.

DAVID: You're not serious.

CALEB: Instead of walking to a nearby tavern, we hop in his car and he drives to this mini-mart, buys a twelve-pack, goes back to the Green Lake parking lot, yells to a couple of his homeys, they get in the car, and we're all drinking beer behind tinted windows, and then one of the guys pulls out some dope and loads a bowl. I'm thinking, gee, we're in public, I could get busted, my wife's home wondering where I am after a miscarriage, and I'm more worried about making contact with some dudes. This is fucked up.

Tyrone says, "What's up, Caleb? You're silent." I say, "Tyrone, sorry, I'm tripping. My wife just had a miscarriage." So Tyrone tells me about his sister and how she had a stillbirth and that I better get home. I say, "Yeah."

In my version of the story I dawdle twenty minutes. Terry calls it an hour and a half. A couple weeks later I'm playing, she comes by, and Tyrone's on the sideline and starts chatting her up, asking if she's watching her "boyfriend." Anyway, she hasn't forgotten.

DAVID: Obviously, it was a serious misstep.

CALEB: I can see us as eighty-year-old grandparents and she'll say, "Remember when I miscarried and you chose beer with Tyrone over coming home to me?"

DAVID: To me, the most interesting aspect of the whole thing is your obsession with entrée into black culture. You wanted to drink a beer with Tyrone, so you shunned Terry. If it had been a white guy, you wouldn't have gone. You wouldn't have felt the same pressure.

CALEB: I've thought about that. I made a conscious decision to get into the culture. I became a regular at Green Lake. I started pushing back. I got sick of the way white guys would get bullied and took it. I didn't want to be like that. When I first started playing there, they're choosing teams and no one picks me, so I call next, and this other guy says, "No, I got next." I say, "We'll run together, then." He says no. Fourteen guys in the gym and ten are playing. I say, "You're not going to pick me up? My game ain't that bad." He says no. This one guy, Nando, says, "Hey, some guys don't pick up white guys." I say, "What if I was six-foot-six?" Nando says, "Wouldn't matter."

DAVID: Nando just pulled you aside and told you this?

CALEB: Yeah. He and I are still cool. So, after a while, I got aggressive, in other people's face. When you get challenged, you puff up and challenge back. I've almost come to blows with Ed Jones. He was talking trash, I called him out, and Ed started threatening me, saying he'd get his piece and leave my daughters without a father. Tyrone and some others got my back, got between us and started threatening Ed. Ed backed down.

○

CALEB: Immediately after graduating from the UW with a degree in poli-sci, Terry worked in supermarkets, hanging up advertising, and she's still with the same company. She became a vice president, then a director of retail sales accounts.

DAVID: What's the company?

CALEB: It became News America Marketing when it was bought by NewsCorp.

DAVID: In other words, Murdoch.

CALEB: In LA she's worked out of the Fox Studios building. She travels a lot: LA, San Fran, New York. She met Henry Kissinger at a party, has ridden in an elevator with Bill O'Reilly.

DAVID: So on some level she's working for Fox News?

CALEB: No. Both her company and Fox News belong to NewsCorp. She negotiates advertising between producers and retailers. If Sara Lee wants product placement in Albertsons, they talk to someone like her.

DAVID: Sure. Just like publishers pay to have books displayed in the front of the store. Is she someone who likes to work?

CALEB: She says no, but if she's not working, she gets restless. She likes aspects of the job, the responsibility and satisfaction. She feels that, well, my friends and I are artists and have relatively stunted careers, but we made a choice not to get a job that demands a certain commitment. I've got friends close to fifty, and they have the typical liberal take: they want the government to pay for their health care and so forth.

DAVID: That's a right-wing caricature of the typical liberal take.

CALEB: They think corporations are greedy and predatory, whereas, to Terry, corporations employ thousands of people, and these people work hard but are well compensated. We have health insurance and security because of her, and it was a choice she made.

DAVID: She thinks you guys are a bunch of spoiled brats?

CALEB: She tells me, "I wanted financial security. That was important to me, and I work my ass off." And she does. She's the ant and we artists are grasshoppers, writing songs and poems and novels as we curse this cold and dark planet.

DAVID: Got it in one.

CALEB: Her job is hard. It's fatiguing and stressful, so she deserves to come home and watch mindless TV and relax with a glass or two of wine.

DAVID: Does she make a good salary?

CALEB: Around one twenty-five, counting bonuses. She flies a lot, so we can take vacations on her frequent flyer miles. What do you make at the UW?

DAVID: Same.

CALEB: One twenty-five and you work six months of the year?

DAVID: I teach two quarters a year. It's more like five months a year.

CALEB: You have to read and prepare, but still, $125,000?

DAVID: Does that seem like a lot?

CALEB: Yes. And you were worried about money in 1996?

DAVID: When I first came to the UW, I was making twenty-seven. Salaries at the UW are pretty bad, due to state cutbacks. The only reason I have a decent salary is I keep getting recruited by other schools. It's like anything: you become more desirable when someone else desires you. My salary went up considerably, from sixty to ninety. Then I got another offer and it went from ninety to one-ten.

CALEB: Amazing.

DAVID: That's what Laurie says. She thinks I have the cushi-
est job in the world, but I've worked unbelievably—

CALEB: Heard it. Heard it.

○

CALEB: In business journals, when a writer touts a company
or stock, at the end of the article there's usually a disclo-
sure saying whether the writer, the writer's employer, or
the writer's family members own the stock, so if there's a
conflict of interest it's transparent. The lit world should be
so forthcoming. The lit community praises the lit community, there's a dearth of constructive criticism, and there's a
fuck of a lot of praise for boring books.

DAVID: You're preachin' to the choir, brother.

CALEB: We need more of Dale Peck's *Hatchet Jobs* and Anis
Shivani's "The 15 Most Overrated Contemporary Ameri-
can Writers." Shivani went after Jhumpa Lahiri and Junot
Díaz and Sharon Olds.

DAVID: That would be just the beginning of my critique.

CALEB: If we can't criticize, we stay in the muck, and the
literary world shrinks proportionately to the culture. Who
trusts or even reads positive reviews? Would you rather
have a positive review read by a hundred people, or a negative review read by a thousand? You wrote about how painful negative reviews were in the past, and now you don't
care. You were inferring, almost, that it's more painful if
some intimate shows disinterest.

DAVID: One of the accomplishments for me of middle age is, boy, can I shrug off criticism. It used to be, I'd get a bad review in the *Orlando Sentinel,* and I'd dwell on it inordinately. Now I literally don't have time. Somebody writes a six-thousand-word attack on *Reality Hunger*? I'm thrilled the book got so deeply under his skin.

○

DAVID: How's Scott Driscoll doing?

CALEB: He read *Reality Hunger.* He's a very good critic. He loves fiction.

DAVID: Yeah, and?

CALEB: He's responsible for that opening of our interview in the *Rumpus,* when I asked, "You began writing fiction; it turned out not to be your forte. Why the attack? Isn't that like an impotent man vowing abstinence?"

DAVID: Only about fifty other reviewers used the same trope. I'd say I'm more like a man in love pointing out to the man on Viagra that he's fucking a sex doll.

CALEB: How long have you been rehearsing that one?

○

DAVID: You're a funny intersection of hippie and military.

CALEB: My dad was in Saigon for a year, and my parents

were in Asia for eight years. He has no clue about art, and she's creative, quasi-bohemian. She knew I smoked pot and kept it from him. My dad won't watch movies about genocide, anything negative, anything "depressing." He's "Who cares about the Holocaust? It's over. Who cares?"

DAVID: He's anti-intellectual, but is he smart?

CALEB: After Cooper Union he got a master's from NYU in engineering. He's very organized.

DAVID: Is your mom intellectual at all?

CALEB: She used to be well-read and big into art. Completely stopped.

DAVID: What books would they be reading? She was reading something when I stopped by.

CALEB: Probably *People* magazine. Their house is a museum. Every *National Geographic* since before 1920. Four sets of encyclopedias. There are probably over five thousand books. The classics: Homer, Shakespeare, Melville. I remember being forced to listen to *Beowulf* when I was ten. My dad, though, has a huge collection of Carter Brown mysteries, Alistair MacLean spy novels, and romance novels. He's addicted to romance.

○

CALEB: In high school I just read mystery, science fiction, and sports magazines, but I did browse our books and the *Nat Geo*s. Not until college and wanting to become a writer did I read. I was getting into philosophy, Christianity.

DAVID: Your book is definitely coming back to me. It deals with those three friends—Mark, Vince, and "you." Still seems like it could be a good book.

CALEB: You're misremembering a little. It was based on Mark and Vince, but I made them into one character whose dad's dead. Both Mark and Vince lost a parent in high school. You said about it, "I'm especially impressed by the narrator's ability to compress his meditations into startling aphorisms, and at crucial moments—sex, love, drugs, religion, nature, death—the prose is joyful, even ecstatic."

DAVID: That sounds like me.

CALEB: You thought it should begin in Seattle, because the first part was slow.

DAVID: Where was the first part set?

CALEB: A small town. The story was set chronologically. You wanted the novel to begin after the father died. You wanted flashbacks.

DAVID: I do remember that. I remember I wanted to steal that line of yours.

CALEB: And I should have let you. Then I could have said, "Gimme a blurb."

○

CALEB: Last night I woke up at four a.m., thinking about your X factor. And mine. I'm fascinated by death, but especially killing. There's no more dramatic moment in life than killing, or watching someone dying. But killing entertains us. Why? Answer that, and you get to suffering. And where we fit in. How do we stop suffering? How do we love? Are you familiar with Haing Ngor and Dith Pran?

DAVID: Of course. In *Swimming to Cambodia*, Spalding Gray talks about how Ngor played Pran in *The Killing Fields*.

CALEB: Both of them thought *The Killing Fields* tamed death, made it palatable. In *Silence of the Lambs* Jodie Foster finds skinned corpses in swamps, but that's okay. That's entertainment. You ever read *A Cambodian Odyssey*?

DAVID: I haven't.

CALEB: Haing Ngor's autobiography, told to someone or other. Ngor witnessed a Khmer Rouge cadre get angry because this pregnant woman wasn't working hard. The cadre took his bayonet, disemboweled her, sliced out her fetus, tied the fetus to a string, and hung it from a porch. There were about a dozen other small, shriveled, shrunken clumps hanging from the porch rafters, and until this moment Ngor hadn't realized they were fetuses.

DAVID: There's nothing I can say.

CALEB: In college I chose art before politics, but I changed. Politics, art, love, life—they converge. Brian Fawcett concluded *Cambodia* by meditating on Prince Sihanouk's words: "The Khmer Rouge withheld the basic human right to be loved." This platitude scores a direct hit on my X factor.

DAVID: I'm sure I sound like a complete asshole, but that's the problem: it's a platitude. It's not taking us anywhere interesting.

◐

CALEB: *(handing David a manuscript)* This is "The Biography of Davy Muth," a Cambodian woman, pronounced
"Dah-vee" but spelled like Davy Crockett. She's been writing her autobiography for twenty years and recently asked
me if I'd help. She lived in Phnom Penh, was a teacher,
had four children and a husband who was a professor at
a military academy. April 17, 1975, rolled around: over
the next weeks she saw her husband loaded onto the back
of a truck—last time she saw him. Her family then splits
up: two of her children go with her sister and mother, and
she takes two. They die—one executed, one poisoned. She
doesn't hear anything about her family until January of
1979, when Vietnam invades. She goes to a refugee camp
in Thailand, is reunited with her other two children. Thai
soldiers rape Cambodians; she and her sister dig holes and
hide every night. She finally made it to Seattle. Through
her story I weave: Why do we kill? Why do we enjoy killing if we think it's fictional? Why are we fascinated with
serial killers? Can this fascination lead to solutions? Can
we develop empathy through imagination to finally arrive
at action?

DAVID: *(looking at the manuscript)* That doesn't sound that far
from my own Iraqi-Afghani-Vietnamese idea.

CALEB: In your writing, you have a hesitancy to judge—
a moral relativism that allows anything into play, and it
comes across as amoral. You're so hesitant.

DAVID: You have a much more public and political imagination than I do. And I'd love to see if I can't burn your village down to the—

CALEB: I—

DAVID: Let me finish, Caleb. It's not as if you're a hugely right-on person who is out there manning the barricades, but you think of yourself as more politically engaged than I am. Okay. Well, I want to investigate that. Even though you're twelve years younger than I am, you remind me, in a way, of my mother and father. You probably think of me as—I don't know—neurotic, overly interior, solipsistic, whatever. But I find you extremely didactic, moralistic, polemical, self-righteous, preachy. Is that unfair? You say I'm hesitant to judge, but—hey—I'm happy to judge anything anytime.

CALEB: You judge subjective taste issues: a book, a movie, a painting, but on moral issues, no.

DAVID: I think of myself, in fact, as trying to scrutinize each choice. Can you think of an example where I'll give someone too much benefit of the doubt?

CALEB: You paint a picture of people taking advantage of their race—the NBA as reparation theater.

DAVID: I would certainly write that book differently now.

CALEB: Your interpretation of Fawcett's *Cambodia* was off. You wrote, essentially, "Brian Fawcett uses juxtaposition as a way to show that mass culture is as insidious as the Khmer Rouge."

DAVID: But in his email to us, he actually seemed to agree with me. Otherwise, there's no point to that book; there's no other way to make sense of the bifurcation of the page into media parables and war atrocity.

CALEB: I just reread *Cambodia*. Your interpretation isn't so far off, but that just means that both you and Fawcett are wrong. Any Cambodian who lived through the Khmer Rouge would not think the invasion of McDonald's and Walmart and TV into their homes is so terrible. That's a Howard Zinn/Noam Chomsky–level analogue. Absurd.

DAVID: "When you ask me if I'm political, what you're really saying is, 'Do you identify your critique of everyday life as a political one?' It seems to me a politics of consciousness and a politics of awareness are so lacking in most of what are considered to be political viewpoints that I'm not sure I want to call it politics. Before I can begin to discuss the kind of questions that people normally call 'politics,' I would have to solve perceptual and mental and emotional confusions that seem to me to so surround every discourse that I certainly haven't gotten anywhere close to 'politics' yet."

CALEB: Who's that?

DAVID: Lethem.

CALEB: Let's talk about *Human Smoke*.

○

DAVID: Nicholson Baker is sympathetic to Quakerism, is essentially a pacifist. And he wanted to give himself the toughest possible case to make for pacifism: World War II. Most people would support the Allied effort to stop the Nazis.

CALEB: Even Chomsky.

DAVID: Baker doesn't, in any way, justify what Hitler did, but he wants to show you Roosevelt's and Churchill's warmongering, their death-dealing. The book is trying to show you that, finally, if Germans die, if Japanese die, if Americans die, if British soldiers die, it's all human smoke. We're all people. We're all mortal beings. That's the book, and it'd be hard to argue otherwise.

CALEB: I'll argue otherwise.

DAVID: You see it differently?

CALEB: Baker showed the warmongering of the Allies, but the book doesn't say, "We're all human smoke." Baker says that despite the degradation war brings, "we must fight. We must stop evil at all costs." And that's the message.

DAVID: It is?

CALEB: In the final scene, two Nazi soldiers are outside a concentration camp. One takes a whiff of the ash in the air and says, "Ahh, human smoke!" This macabre image contradicts your forced metaphor.

DAVID: You're right to focus on that paragraph, but to me you're reading it way too literally. If that's all he was saying, why would he even have bothered to write the book? Why did the book receive so many reviews that were beyond negative? The entire strategy of the book—interpolating hundreds of paragraphs, all from different sources—militates against your reading.

CALEB: Baker illustrates the moral ambiguities of the Allies, but in no way does he make a case against World War II.

DAVID: Jews in ovens. Jews as candles. We've been there a million times.

CALEB: Six million times.

DAVID: Baker is trying to take you someplace stranger and, to me, more interesting. Am I a moral relativist and are you a moral absolutist—is that what this is about?

CALEB: I struggle with that myself.

DAVID: I really like that line of Goethe's: "I've never heard of a crime I couldn't imagine committing myself." To me, one way that human beings can become better, or at least that art can serve people, is if the writer or the artist shows how flawed he or she actually is. Basically, the royal road to salvation, for me, lies through an artist saying very uncompromising things about himself. And through reading that relentless investigation, the reader will understand something surprising about himself. I always come back to the idea that we're all bozos on this bus. If my work has value, which I have to believe it does, it's in the realm of helping—or more like forcing—other human beings to confront their/our shared humanity/flawedness. If every single person in the world read my books—

Caleb laughs.

DAVID: First of all, I'd be richer than that guy you know who wrote *The Art of Racing in the Rain*—

CALEB: Garth Stein—

DAVID: —which would be a very good thing. And second of all, people would not, I swear to god, go around killing one another, because they'd stop thinking that evil is "out there." That's why it's so important to me to empty out Franzen. Everything he writes is in the service of fighting off any insight into himself and locating instead all shade and shadow elsewhere, out there, the next precinct over.

CALEB: As opposed to evil inside.

DAVID: You know it.

CALEB: The common man will be evil. Voltaire: "Those who can make you believe absurdities can make you commit atrocities." Stanley Milgram added the exclamation point with his experiments. Yeah, no duh, people are like this. Normal people will submit to authority and become sociopaths.

DAVID: Right. And, boy, is Franzen always on his high moral horse. He, to me, is utter anathema, whereas Wallace, at his best, was always going deeper into himself, flaying himself alive in order for us to understand ourselves better. That's a pretty big fucking accomplishment.

○

DAVID: I'm your former teacher, I'm a much more established writer than you are, but you seem much more certain of yourself.

CALEB: I tell Terry that I'm the king of uncertainty.

DAVID: You are?

CALEB: I'm so not certain, but when I say something I don't incessantly qualify it with doubt. Inside—inside, I'm uncertain.

DAVID: That's a relief, and it makes me believe even more in you as a writer. It's that Graham Greene line: "When we are not sure, we are alive."

CALEB: What do you think about Greene?

DAVID: He has a Manichean view of the universe: good and evil.

CALEB: Sounds pretty certain to me.

○

CALEB: When Toni Morrison was nominated for a National Book Award and didn't win, did she really say to a judge, "Thank you for ruining my life"?

DAVID: According to my former teacher, yes.

CALEB: It seems beneath her.

DAVID: Why would it be beneath her? She's just like anyone else.

○

DAVID: Are you an atheist?

CALEB: I consider myself an Einsteinian agnostic.

DAVID: I'm an atheist. Tomorrow I might get hit by a bolt of lightning and change my view, but I'm living my life as if we're animals and we're here on earth, more evolved than a muskrat but not essentially different. My friend Robert, who's Catholic, says the only thing that interests him is eschatology.

CALEB: The study of shit?

DAVID: Not scatology. Eschatology.

CALEB: Oops.

DAVID: Dostoevsky wondering endlessly, "Is there a god?" "If there is no god, how do we live a moral life?" "What happens after we die?" These are children's questions. I'd rather talk about why we kill. What's the difference between a Hindu god and an Incan god? You're all deluded. What does Bertrand Russell call it? The celestial teapot. If you want to believe this teapot is magical, fine, but it's no more meaningful than believing that a curtain rod carries divinity.

CALEB: You hear about the dyslexic, insomniac agnostic?

DAVID: I probably have, but I forget the punch line.

CALEB: He stayed up all night wondering whether there's a dog.

○

CALEB: At family gatherings, I come across as a moronic dude who likes to drink beer. I'm accident-prone, I spill things, I break dishes, and I like sports. There's a certain pretense on your part. You're the artist above it all.

DAVID: Well, sure. I'm very pretentious, but I'm not a snob.

CALEB: In *Black Planet* you were. You had two season tickets to Sonics games and had trouble finding someone to go with you. You advertised, and then Henry offered to buy six tickets. Then you dismissed Henry because he worked at Elma Lanes bowling alley. You even wrote to begin the paragraph, "I'm a snob." You missed an opportunity.

DAVID: I know. I agree.

CALEB: Henry represents the world.

DAVID: If it turned out bad, it would have been better. Two hours of painfully literal conversation.

CALEB: Again, you're dismissing Henry as if everything will go over his head. And it might have, but stuff like this makes me wonder if you even want to understand people at "ground level." Forget about the sixty to seventy percent of humanity struggling for basic comforts, food and shelter and survival; they have reasons why they don't read. But even in America, of the population that can read and does read, many don't read literary works. They're not all morons. Why would they read David Shields if David Shields doesn't want to hang out with them? Walk through a casino—look at everyone putting money in slots. Hang out in a dive bar.

○

CALEB: Terry likes that I don't like porn.

DAVID: What man doesn't like porn?

CALEB: I wouldn't say I don't like it—I'm fascinated by it; I enjoy watching erotic images—but I've spoken out against it, too. Prostitution in Cambodia's a lot different than in Vegas. I believe humans should be free to seek their own abysses. Anything is permissible as long as there's no outside harm. I try to apply that to porn.

DAVID: How does Terry know whether you do or don't like porn?

CALEB: She's my wife. I don't have porn. Okay, I have about ten Chinese *Playboy*s from Hong Kong. They're almost thirty years old. My mom bought them last time she was in Hong Kong.

DAVID: What's that all about?

CALEB: My mom's—well, a book of her own.

○

CALEB: I stopped watching the Mariners because of Josh Lueke.

DAVID: Is he the one who hit his wife?

CALEB: That's Julio Mateo. The Mariners released him.

DAVID: Lueke raped a girl?

CALEB: He was charged with rape. Lueke's DNA was on the anal swab. He pled to the obscure lesser felony of "kidnapping with violence" and served time. He was in the minors, and I told Terry if the Mariners move him up from AAA, I'm done with the Mariners. He made the team, so I'm done, for what it's worth. First year I've been in Seattle and not attended at least one game.

DAVID: How did it come out that it was anal rape?

CALEB: Just look on the web.

DAVID: Is he that great of a player?

CALEB: He throws ninety-five, has potential. He's young.

DAVID: He's a reliever?

CALEB: Uh-huh.

DAVID: I wonder how they justified that. "Let's give him a second chance"?

CALEB: The Mariners fired the scout who recruited him.

DAVID: It was the scout's fault?

CALEB: Lueke's public statement was, more or less, "I made a mistake—talk to my lawyer."

○

DAVID: In *The Fall* there's a Frenchman who welcomes and loves all humanity despite being surrounded by a war machine. One day he opens the door and is greeted by a bayonet to his gut. Camus then describes a woman forced to choose which child she wants executed.

CALEB: When did Styron write *Sophie's Choice*?

DAVID: Twenty years after *The Fall*. I'd take any sentence of *The Fall* over all of *Sophie's Choice*. In that Camus paragraph I get everything. I don't need four hundred pages of *Sophie's Choice*. The student of mine who "shot a dude": you want a whole book about that. I'd say, "Just give me the line."

CALEB: I don't want a book, but I want more. Prison life must be very dramatic.

DAVID: What about prison life interests you so much?

CALEB: They're doing time. People who aren't very reflective all of a sudden have nothing to do but meditate on life, death, crime, punishment, family, and pain. Everyone in prison has a story. There's murder, capital punishment, redemption, recidivism, justice.

DAVID: Not everyone in prison has shot someone. Some people just wrote a bad check.

CALEB: You hear about the rapper who went to prison?

DAVID: Uh-oh.

CALEB: "Rhyme and Punishment."

○

CALEB: I'm against the death penalty, but with an asterisk. I'm more against releasing the Lockerbie bomber after only eight years. The Scottish prime minister let him go because he had terminal cancer. It was the "humanitarian thing to do." He lived the rest of his life, as a hero, in Libya. That's cruel and unusual treatment of all the victims. Anders Breivik, the Norwegian guy who killed seventy or so people, has a possibility of parole in twenty-one years. Life imprisonment is superior to execution, but execution is superior to setting Anders Breivik free.

DAVID: Now who's the moral relativist?

○

CALEB: *(into DVR)* It's Friday, around noon, and we're driving to the town of Skykomish for lunch.

DAVID: Are Khamta and his wife trying for a second kid?

CALEB: They weren't at first, but now they are. She's three or four years older than he is; I think she's forty-one.

DAVID: Is she a Buddhist?

CALEB: Khamta is only mildly Buddhist. Julie's traveled and she's interested in Laotian culture, but that probably had little to do with her marrying Khamta, who left Laos when he was seven, stayed in a refugee camp, and was one of two families sponsored by the Methodist church in Coupeville.

DAVID: What does Julie do?

CALEB: She's a photographer. She works for department stores, and she's working now at McChord Air Force Base for some big project. She went to Peru and did a nice collage of children. . . . Okay, here's the meth house we visited last night.

DAVID: It's brutal.

CALEB: It's an absolute sty. You wouldn't have wanted to stay there.

DAVID: I can survive anything.

○

DAVID: When I gave that reading at Suzzallo, I didn't recognize you. I don't think I'd seen you for—what?—fifteen years if not more.

CALEB: From 1991 to 2008! Seventeen years. We'd exchanged a few emails.

DAVID: I remembered you as having long dark locks—down to your shoulders if not longer. Very dramatic. You looked like a heavy-metal drummer; it was a big part of your identity, I always thought. It was interesting to see the photos of you at your house—how your hair receded year by year. When did you join the bald club?

CALEB: About ten years ago. I didn't want to look like Gallagher.

DAVID: Bald with long hair. Gotcha. Ridiculous.

CALEB: Even short hair bald looks dumb. The skin yarmulke.

DAVID: Shaved is the way to go. Just admit who and where you are in life.

CALEB: It's easier.

DAVID: In my thirties I was endlessly trying to finesse my hair so it'd look decent.

CALEB: I started losing my hair in my late twenties. I thought long hair was an asset with the ladies. Actually, for every one woman the hair attracted, it repelled ten. Terry said she wouldn't have looked twice at me had we met in my long-hair days. The shaved head opens up the widest spectrum of options for the balding guy in the dating world, unless your head is shaped like a potato.

DAVID: If I had my druthers, I'd have more hair. Baldness ages one. And a lot of the people Laurie has had crushes on had long hair—Cat Stevens, James Taylor, Todd Rundgren, Taylor Kitsch.

CALEB: Taylor Kitsch?

DAVID: The kid in *Friday Night Lights*. It's nothing I think about overly much. I shaved my head by 1997, early forties.

CALEB: I probably started to shave regularly when I turned thirty.

DAVID: Now I do it practically every other day.

○

DAVID: So this is the little town of Skykomish?

CALEB: Burlington Northern, the railroad, leaked oil or pollutants into the water supply underground, and the whole town was dug up. There are two restaurants, but only one was ever open at any given time, and the grass you see used to be twenty-foot-deep pits.

DAVID: Every building was simply picked up and moved?

CALEB: Or razed. The structural engineers had to figure it all out.

Train whistle.

DAVID: Will this be endlessly long?

CALEB: Could be five cars, could be a hundred. Barouh was with his girfriend and their son and dog down the mountain, straddling the track, not paying attention; the stereo's blasting, and they didn't hear the train whistle. The train nailed the bed of the truck, killed the dog instantly.

DAVID: How dumb do you have to be?

CALEB: Every time Khamta and I come to a train track, we shout out, "Barouh! Baroooooouh!"

DAVID: Is he an oblivious guy?

CALEB: Unofficially, he's got ADD. He's hyper and always

focused on something else. Whenever I call he says, "I'm busy—can I call you right back?"

DAVID: Who was injured besides the dog?

CALEB: The girlfriend and the son were airlifted by helicopter to Harborview. She was messed up, missed six months of work. The son just had bumps and bruises.

DAVID: Barouh had no injury?

CALEB: Just scrapes. Didn't even see a doctor, but that was the final straw. The girlfriend left.

. . .

Here we are—the Cascadia Inn.

○

DAVID: Laurie has what she calls "cellular issues"—periodic biopsies, mini-scares about dysplasia, her cells' repair mechanism—but she doesn't really fill me in on to what degree she's worried, whereas I would tend to want to talk about it.

CALEB: Maybe she'd like you to ask.

DAVID: Believe me, I ask. She's John Wayne: strong, silent type.

WAITRESS: Hi. Two?

DAVID: Two. Do you have wireless?

WAITRESS: Yes.

DAVID: Oh, good. Let me get out my laptop.

CALEB: So Laurie's okay?

DAVID: We think so. She's now a health fiend. How's Terry's health?

CALEB: Three babies, three miscarriages. Basically, she was pregnant for five-plus years. I mean, she's beautiful. She loves taking walks, works out at home with aerobics videos.

DAVID: Who was that jumping up and down on the bed back at your house?

CALEB: Gia; she's the middle one.

DAVID: Pretty cute. How about the other kids—are they as sweet-tempered?

CALEB: I've won the lottery three times. You said you didn't enjoy the first couple years of parenthood.

DAVID: I struggled a little bit. Did you not?

CALEB: Struggle? A little, but for every negative there're three or four positives.

WAITRESS: Today's specials are a Denver omelet and the chicken salad sandwich. Coffee?

○

DAVID: Do you know how to dive into a swimming pool?

CALEB: Sure.

DAVID: It's something I've never learned to do.

CALEB: You can't?

DAVID: I can sort of do it, but it's basically a belly flop.

CALEB: You've never dove from a diving board?

DAVID: It's embarrassing, but I've never learned.

CALEB: You just jump headfirst. Let me show you a bungee jump.

DAVID: Computer's yours.

CALEB: YouTube: Victoria Falls, Zimbabwe. Gimme a couple seconds. *(plays video)*

DAVID: Were you afraid?

CALEB: I was more afraid of chickening out.

DAVID: How do you get back up?

CALEB: A second person came down on a winch, latched onto me, and back up we went.

DAVID: Are you proud you did it? Did you learn something?

CALEB: Conquering fear—all that bullshit.

DAVID: How did you get to the moment where you jumped off?

CALEB: I'd made the choice the previous day, signed up, and paid ninety bucks. I imagined not doing it, and between the two, I had to jump. The guy counted down, "Five, four, three, two, bungee!"

DAVID: Can I see the bungee jump again?

CALEB: Sure. *(replays)*

DAVID: It's hard to imagine what's in your body, your heart—I don't know how you control that. You must have felt so relieved. Were you just hanging there afterward?

CALEB: For about five minutes, upside down, waiting for this guy to drop on the winch. The whole way back he told me about how they paid him a dollar a day to risk his life.

WAITRESS: Are we ready?

CALEB: Yes. I'll have the Denver omelet.

WAITRESS: The cook has stopped serving breakfast.

○

CALEB: You want to see a video of [Terry's sister] Tracy telling a dirty joke?

DAVID: What do you think?

CALEB: Okay, context: This is last May. We're in Mexico for Tracy's wedding and telling jokes at dinner.

YouTube video:

Caleb: Lights, camera, action.

Tracy: Why are girls so bad at math?

Jan (mother-in-law): Girls?

Tracy: (holds index finger two inches from her thumb) Because men keep telling them this is eight inches.

All: (laughter)

DAVID: Do Terry and Tracy get along?

CALEB: Best friends. Terry has three friends: her mom, her sister, and my sister. Tracy's always over.

WAITRESS: *(giving David the bill and credit card)* Here you go. This one's for us and this one can be your souvenir.

DAVID: Thanks a lot.

WAITRESS: You're welcome a lot.

She leaves.

DAVID: So if we came into town for lunch again, or dinner, would this be where we go? I liked it. They're really friendly.

○

DAVID: The waitress saying, "Pie like grandma makes it," the American flag, the salute to our troops, the motorcycles parked like horses outside—I dig it all.

CALEB: Imagine that's your house.

DAVID: I could do it. My neighbor, Sandy, is a lawyer in her mid-sixties. Her daughter has a lesbian partner, and the two of them are raising a kid in Bloomington, Indiana. Sandy is selling her house and moving there to be a grandmother. I could do that. If Natalie were living in Indiana, raising a family, and Laurie and I decided to move there to be near her, I'd be fine. Part of me pretends to crave New York, but I really don't. I'm an incredibly simple person. This is beautiful country.

○

CALEB: Eula Biss dedicated *Notes from No Man's Land* to her future son. After the interview, we chatted and I asked if she had had the son yet. She had. I asked if she was going to have another. She was leaning toward no. She teaches at Northwestern and feared she wouldn't have time to write. The more successful the writer becomes, the less time for other things. I wondered if I could make these sacrifices for my art. Publication, attention, success—how does it change you?

DAVID: To be honest, the last thing I ever feel is "successful." There's no guarantee; every book is—

CALEB: You win the NBCC award, like Eula did: your next book's guaranteed.

DAVID: Not really.

CALEB: You may say "no guarantee." Let me tell you about "no guarantee."

DAVID: When Laurie and I had the debate whether to have a second child, I had published four books. *Remote* had just come out. It's not as if *Remote* set the world on fire, but it did get a lot of attention. I was an associate professor, with tenure, at the UW. I had found my métier: I was working on *Black Planet* and I thought, man—

Train whistle blows.

DAVID: Baroooouh!

It does feel selfish. Everything is selfish. If you have four children, you're doing it for yourself. You're doing it for them, but you're doing it for your own self-fulfillment. I feel okay about it. It's not as if, you know—did I let Laurie down?

CALEB: You want the kid entering the world to a welcome.

DAVID: I'm sure, if we had had a second child, it would have brought greater complexity and joy into our lives. It was mainly a financial thing.

CALEB: If you knew you'd be making a hundred and twenty-five grand in the future—

DAVID: I was making about thirty-five, and Laurie was making twenty-five, and I wanted to be able to pay for Natalie's education. . . . Ah, here's the meth lab house.

○

DAVID: I can see how, in the construction business, cocaine must be a bit of an occupational hazard.

CALEB: I worked in Snohomish with this Coupeville guy who blew almost his entire paycheck on crack. He'd cook rock on the job. Smart guy, though. I'm in college and by the time I graduate he's leading a crew, youngest guy on the job, but loved the drug. Then got into meth. He's now doing time in Monroe. Barouh's stayed away from that kind of trouble. . . . Okay, we got Barouh's map. Let's see, Highway 2—this trail takes us to Dorothy Lake.

DAVID: We have to drive, then hike?

CALEB: Seven miles of bad dirt road, then an hour hike. Here's my Washington State Parks pass.

DAVID: Is it a tough hike?

CALEB: A lot of up and down.

DAVID: That's fine.

CALEB: A man's hike!

DAVID: A mile each way?

CALEB: Two.

DAVID: Basically, with my back, I can't do a lot of bending, but I'm up for exploring.

○

Driving very slowly on a U.S. Forest Service dirt road.

CALEB: How do you say it?

DAVID: Deus ex machina—god from the machine. In ancient Greek plays, a god would descend from above the stage and come to the rescue.

CALEB: Sometimes I watch TV with Terry, and every time a deus ex machina pops up to save the day and get the writer out of a jam, I point this out. She tells me to shut up and enjoy the show. *(phone rings)* Speak of the devil.

○

CALEB: Did my mother hug you yesterday?

DAVID: Maybe she craves touch.

CALEB: Terry's parents are divorced and remarried, so I have two fathers-in-law. My mother freaks them both out with her hugging.

DAVID: Don't they give her a little leeway?

CALEB: It still freaks them out.

○

CALEB: George Bush is not really evil.

DAVID: He's not?

CALEB: I would say not.

DAVID: You don't think what he did in Iraq is evil?

CALEB: And I imagine you think Cheney is even—

DAVID: Of course.

CALEB: My friend Vince and I were talking about George Bush. He listed the usual: no weapons of mass destruction, oil, Halliburton, revenge for his father, and then he said that even though he's against capital punishment, he would have liked to see George Bush assassinated. That's just odd.

DAVID: I very strongly want Bush to feel the awfulness of what he's done. I wanted *Checkpoint*—

CALEB: —*Checkpoint*?

DAVID: —Nicholson Baker's fantasy about Bush getting assassinated. I wanted it to end with Bush dead.

CALEB: Hillary Clinton signed on. The U.S. didn't do it alone. It was multilateral; a lot of nations signed on.

DAVID: Not really.

CALEB: Bush is many things, but he ain't "evil."

DAVID: He's the embodiment of evil.

CALEB: In that chapter of yours, you portray him as likable on the airplane.

DAVID: I say that someone else found him likable, and in another chapter I try to find a connection between some of his minor character flaws and my own. It's a literary gesture. . . . Do you know the names of these mountains? They're so beautiful.

CALEB: We'd have to grab the map.

DAVID: I just don't see how the killing of tens of thousands of Iraqi civilians—how is George Bush not evil? Do you think the Iraq War was justified?

CALEB: Was Hillary Clinton evil for supporting the Iraq War?

DAVID: I see what you mean. At what point does it go all the way down?

CALEB: For George Bush to be evil you have to assume that he knew, with absolute certainty, that they were all straw-man arguments. That some aide said, "Mr. President, we've found no weapons." And Bush said, "Then we have to lie so we can go to war against Iraq and I don't care how many Iraqi civilians we kill."

DAVID: I would say that's pretty close to what happened, although of course it would never be spelled out that explicitly. I'm sure you've seen the supposedly funny video [that the Bush administration produced for a White House correspondents' dinner] of Bush trying and failing to find weapons of mass destruction. Looking in a closet: "Can't find any weapons of mass destruction here!" Looking under the bed: "Can't find any weapons there!" Ha ha. You don't think there was at a bare minimum a willful ignorance on Bush's part? The moment 9/11 happened, Bush, Cheney, and Rumsfeld went to the CIA and said, almost literally, "Find us evidence to link Saddam to this event. Just find it." It's pretty clear to me Bush doesn't have a conscience.

CALEB: Do you think he's a psychopath?

DAVID: I wrote that Bush chapter as a conscious attempt to understand a person who daily just absolutely made me crazy. I tried to ask myself, "What points of connection can I make with him?" Because he's unable to make any points of connection with any person who's not in his very gilded cage. Would you at least agree that he's a very, very immoral politician?

CALEB: There's ambiguity and dubiousness to his moral character.

DAVID: Did you vote for him?

CALEB: Gore. Kerry. Obama.

DAVID: You see Bush as simply misguided?

CALEB: I find him genuine.

DAVID: Remember Karla Faye Tucker?

CALEB: Executed when Bush was governor.

DAVID: Bush was asked, "What do you think Karla Faye Tucker would say if she could speak to you?" Bush said, *(nasal tone)* "Help me! Help me!" That, to me, is evil.

CALEB: How familiar are you with that case?

DAVID: Not very.

CALEB: She did it.

DAVID: She did? How do you know?

CALEB: Death penalty cases rivet me. She and her boyfriend went to rob a house and ended up killing this guy with a hammer and a pickaxe. After noticing a girl hiding in the room, Karla killed her with the pickaxe; she embedded multiple blows. Later she said the killing made her feel multiple orgasms.

DAVID: Thank god for small pleasures.

CALEB: She was into drugs and prostitution. Now, she should be in prison for life, sentenced to death by old age, no perks, but that's a different argument. Everything they brought up afterward—her redemption, her conversion to Christianity—is all bullshit. There was no debate of guilt or innocence, and if that issue's gone, then if you're for the death penalty, you should have no remorse. And if you're against it, then come up with better reasons than "she con-verted" or "she truly feels sorry."

○

CALEB: Would you call Obama evil because he's continuing the war in Afghanistan and bombing Libya?

DAVID: I get it. It's a continuum. But killing for simple political—

CALEB: There's a difference between willingness to commit collateral damage versus the willingness to target civilians.

DAVID: And I think this willingness is pretty high with Bush and Cheney.

CALEB: I'd agree. Still, anyone who thinks Bush is "evil" does so out of political bias.

DAVID: I'm no Obama or Hillary or Bill fan, if that's what you're saying. People who kill for political gain—

CALEB: Nothing wrong with cynicism.

○

CALEB: Why didn't we just drop a bomb on Mount Fuji?

DAVID: In '45?

CALEB: A few people lived in the mountains. Nothing like Hiroshima and Nagasaki. We could have sent a message: "We have the bomb. We can waste your cities." If they didn't surrender, we could have dropped a bomb on one of their sparsely populated islands, kill a few hundred people, but not seventy thousand. They'd have gotten the message.

DAVID: You're backforming history.

CALEB: Here's a genocidal dictator, Saddam Hussein, who killed Kurds and Marsh Arabs. He sent his people to die in an absurd war against Iran—U.S.-backed, I know, but Hussein went too far. People on the far right think it's a closed case. Their reasoning is not completely off. They found chemical weapons. He was saber-rattling, acting as if he had weapons, kicking inspectors out. He'd been given many chances. *Many* chances.

DAVID: So you actually supported the war?

CALEB: I thought the cons outweighed the pros, but I did see pros.

DAVID: We're taking slightly different positions than I thought we would. I would have thought you'd have gotten on your high moral horse about the war. What did you think of Christopher Hitchens's waterboarding article?

CALEB: A pompous screed. Of course waterboarding is torture, but so is cleaning up vomit, watching *Glee,* or going to Disneyland. He never was in danger.

DAVID: He's a pussy?

CALEB: The Taliban take five guys, pick one, make the other four watch as they pull out nails, flay, and decapitate. Then they ask the other four if they'd like to talk. That's torture. Enhanced interrogation? At Guantánamo they made prisoners listen to the Barney theme song.

DAVID: I love that song.

CALEB: Van Halen and Metallica and Barney 24/7. Or they'd

take a little meat, vegetables, and potatoes, blend it into a disgusting mush, and serve it. Hitchens's essay would have been a lot different had he written about sitting in a room, listening to Barney, and eating mush. Guantánamo's no resort, but those prisoners play soccer.

○

At the trailhead.

CALEB: *(to DVR)* Friday, September 30th, David Shields and Caleb Powell are at the beginning of the trail to Dorothy Lake in the Cascade Mountains. Here's a brief tourism pitch for the state of Washington: Parks and Forestry does a pretty good job maintaining the trails. For thirty bucks you can visit unlimited for a year. The pass generates a lot of revenue for the parks. I think they've sold over 500,000 passes so far. The mountains are gorgeous. According to the sign, Dorothy Lake is a mile and a half away. I think it's longer.

DAVID: How does anyone know we have the pass?

CALEB: It's on the rearview mirror. Cars without the pass risk a ticket. . . . Return to Hitchens and torture and evil.

DAVID: Hitchens has learned nothing from the history of war. Any war can be defended. "Tyranny." "Communism." "Fascism." Just as I can harm you only as an act of self-defense, a nation ought to fight only when directly threatened. 9/11 wasn't the first strike of an air war. To treat it as such was wrong. My ruling principle is "First do no harm."

CALEB: I don't think we should have gone to Iraq. I just think the pro-war crowd had a valid argument. And Hitler's justification wasn't Churchill's.

DAVID: I like that moment in *Fahrenheit 9/11* when Michael Moore asks various congressmen if their sons and daughters are serving in Iraq. Am I willing to serve in the armed forces or send Natalie to Iraq or Afghanistan or Libya? Of course not.

CALEB: Me neither.

DAVID: Must not be very necessary, then. And that's why World War II was such an interesting case.

CALEB: I'd have felt compelled to enlist.

DAVID: I hope I would have, too. At some point philosophical ambiguity becomes moral cowardice.

CALEB: Thoreau said, "I prefer the philanthropy of Captain [John] Brown to that philanthropy which neither shoots nor liberates me."

DAVID: Right, but there isn't a country in the world the U.S. should now be at war with.

CALEB: The only legitimate reason to intervene is for humanitarian reasons, to stop suffering.

DAVID: Caleb! Can't you hear how double-speak that sounds?

CALEB: Real life is contradictory.

○

CALEB: The hike's up and down all the way, but not too steep. Let me take a picture. In your sunglasses, you look like a spy.

DAVID: About twenty years ago, I went through a Hitchens phase. I love his long essay on Isaiah Berlin: he shows how Berlin's devotion to ambiguity in literature and philosophy wound up turning him into someone who waffled in real life. He couldn't say no to LBJ and supported the Vietnam War. It's a nice reading of Berlin, and I would take that critique, turn it 180 degrees, and apply it to Hitchens.

His father was career British Navy, Hitchens never saw any action, he's incredibly bellicose and opportunistic, and his entire career—from attacks on Clinton to Kissinger to female comedians to God to supporting the Iraq War—is held together by one thread: what places Christopher Hitchens in the center of conflict?

CALEB: Even when he's wrong, he engages the opposition and does his reading. For him to go after Mother Teresa, I'm down with that. I wrote an essay that questioned Rushdie, self-censorship, the media double standard that attacks Christianity but won't defend a Danish cartoonist. Hitchens beat me to it, though—covering the same territory in a piece for the *Nation*. My editor paid me a kill fee. She told me it was in my best interest that no editor or publisher read my article. Some women have balls; she wasn't one of them.

○

CALEB: There's an argument to be made, and Cheney has been making it, that the Iraq invasion helped bring about the Arab Spring.

DAVID: It's just too easy to play fast and loose with other people's lives like that.

CALEB: I half agree with you. I can't imagine losing a daughter to a bomb in the name of collateral damage. NPR had a show, "Widows of Afghanistan." One woman had lost her husband and four children in a missile attack. The entire interview was her bawling. . . . Hey, this is a nice waterfall. I'm going to take a bunch of pictures.

DAVID: It's really beautiful. Did you read that book by Samantha Power?

CALEB: *A Problem from Hell.*

DAVID: She looks at genocide, from Armenia to Bosnia to Rwanda, and how we fail to act. She makes a case that action could prevent atrocity, and I think she's had a huge influence on how Obama—

CALEB: That could be good or bad. I think a Taliban-type government does not do wonders for their people.

DAVID: I disagree with Power. The U.S. has a lot of people who need saving. Forty million people don't have health care. I'd rather take all that money overseas and bring it back here. This whole country is in danger of becoming Third World.

CALEB: America a Third World country? My ass. David Shields, meet Dar es Salaam, Karachi, Manila, and Kampala. Seattle has one homeless for every twenty middle class; Cambodia has one middle class for every twenty dirt-poor quasi-homeless.

DAVID: You looked that up?

CALEB: I'm a *World Almanac* guy. The letter of the stat might be off, but the spirit nails it.

○

DAVID: Natalie went to TOPS, an "alternative" public school, for kindergarten through fifth grade. For a while it was a great school, supposedly among the best or at least "highest-performing" elementary schools in the state, even the country. Every parent was required to volunteer thirty hours a year. Many parents gave much more. I'd come in to Natalie's class and talk about themes in Jerry Spinelli or *Junie B. Jones* or whatever. I gave a class on Ichiro. It was a kick. Then the school district came to resent that there was this school of mainly white, educated, professional, UW-ish parents who had taken a public school and made it a model. They brought in different teachers, a black principal, bused in Asian-immigrant, black, and Hispanic kids, most of whose parents didn't even pretend to be interested in fulfilling the volunteer requirement. They didn't have the time, the flexibility at work, they didn't speak the language, or they just didn't place a very high value on education, if that isn't too racist a thing to say.

Every week I was giving part of my day to take a kid out of class, a bad actor whose parents refused to discipline him, and try to bring him up to speed. The school became obsessed with "attacking the gap"—the achievement gap between blacks and whites. Not by bringing black kids up to where the white kids were, but by willfully bringing the scores of the white kids down. It was a revisitation

of everything I found so aggravating about my PC childhood. I yanked Natalie out of the school and sent her to
a private middle school Laurie and I couldn't afford. I'm
embarrassed, because I'm privileged and white, but when
the rubber hit the road, I wanted what was best for my
daughter.

CALEB: At Ava's school we have to pay $2,300 a year for kin-
dergarten. Kids whose income falls below a certain level
don't pay, and they also get free hot breakfast and lunch.

DAVID: You guys can afford it.

CALEB: I'm not complaining. It's not the kids' fault their parents are single parents, foreigners, low-income. Kids who
otherwise wouldn't have a better diet: their families can be
helped financially. I'm okay with socialism as charity. Not
as social engineering.

I taught ESL for eight years, and no matter if it was in
Abu Dhabi or Korea or Brazil, I'd teach the students who
came to learn. In the UAE I'd teach three or four students
who sat at the front of the class with pen and paper. I wasn't
going to bother with the students preparing for life as a
government sinecure. That'd hurt the better students.

DAVID: I'm okay with that. If there are thirty-two kids in
Ava's class, and Ava isn't learning anything because the
teacher's spending half of her time teaching Gabriel to sit
in his seat, I'm not cool with that.

CALEB: These mountains—I'm going to take some pictures . . .

◌

CALEB: What is it with you and Ichiro?

DAVID: What are you—a big anti-Ichiro guy?

CALEB: I respect him as a ballplayer.

DAVID: Not as a person?

CALEB: There's a scene in *Lost in Translation* when a Japanese man is asked a question through an interpreter and responds at length. The interpreter turns and says, "He agrees."

DAVID: So?

CALEB: That's what I think is happening with Ichiro. He just wants to take a shower. You ascribe poetry to him which I don't think exists.

DAVID: Have you read the Ichiro book? You read all those quotes and you still think he's not up to something interesting? You don't think he's pushing back quite hard against the melodrama of American sports clichés?

CALEB: No.

DAVID: If I'm overreading him slightly here and there, then what the hell, you know, 'cause otherwise there wouldn't have been a book.

○

CALEB: There are inferior and superior cultures.

DAVID: Wow. You're saying that as a fact?

CALEB: It is a fact.

DAVID: I basically agree, but I don't think you're supposed to say that.

CALEB: That should change. I've got to be careful with semantics, because culture and race overlap, so let me qualify. Racism creates unequal cultures and becomes self-perpetuating. Don't get me wrong: I love cultures. Mix, integrate, travel, discover, but the idea that cultures are equal is nonsense. People have equal rights and abilities. Cultures aren't equal, though. A culture of wealth is, by definition, not the same as a culture of poverty. Wealth correlates with better life expectancy, lower infant mortality, less violence. U.S. Southern culture in 2011 is superior to U.S. Southern culture in 1832. European culture of today is superior to the Europe of the Dark Ages.

DAVID: How do you define culture?

CALEB: Society's collective modus vivendi: what a given people generally believe and practice. "The critique of culture is confronted with the last stage in the dialectic of culture and barbarism."

DAVID: Adorno.

CALEB: Preceding the oft-quoted "To write a poem after Auschwitz is barbaric." Adorno isn't saying, "Don't write poems." He's questioning the conflict between the culture of poetry and the culture of barbarism: namely, solve Auschwitz, then solve art.

DAVID: That's wrong. That's not how art works. You don't solve questions first, then turn to art to embody the answers. The art is where you investigate the questions.

CALEB: But Adorno's asking, Does art offer solutions? If so, then you solve both. And that, I think, gets to what I'm trying to say. In other words, when a society, a culture, collectively believes that it's okay to butcher Jews or purchase and own another person, that society is inferior. When a society believes that it's okay to force sex on a woman, sell a woman, stone her for adultery, rape her, or kill her for honor, that society is inferior. Culture underlies society.

DAVID: I wouldn't call that culture, but politics and governance.

CALEB: Politics reflects society. In most places an honor killing is treated as murder. Pakistan reports eight hundred honor killings a year. Hey, it's dangerous territory, because when race and culture correlate, then to attack one you attack the other. By confronting culture, you risk being branded a racist. That's a risk I'll take. It's an argument worth having. Oscar Wilde went to prison for two years for sodomy. The British court that condemned him came from an inferior culture.

Asians and Africans are equal, but their cultures can't be. No cultures are. Cultures evolve; politics change. In India and China, men outnumber women by large margins in some regions because of gender-selective abortion. I'm quantifying existentially. The Mayans and Incans and the followers of Abraham sacrificed children. The Korowai in New Guinea practice cannibalism today. The Yanamamo kill firstborn females. The Jivaro male must kill another man to be initiated into adulthood. In some cultures, you're not a woman until your aunt slices your clit off.

DAVID: I support reparations for African Americans—forty acres and a mule?—but I'm somewhat ambivalent about affirmative action. Why are so many African Americans still poor, and why do so many grow up without a father? Is it post-slavery stress disorder? History moves—1865,

1964, 2008—but does the clock ever run out? Obama has said as much, or at least tried to ask questions along these lines. I tend to romanticize the work ethic of Vietnamese, Koreans, Jews, whereas other cultures—Hispanic, African American—don't appear to place quite as much value on advancing up the social ladder. Can one say that? Why couldn't one say that?

CALEB: It's not race. It's not ethnicity. It's the culture. One culture dominates another: the oppressed has a disadvantage. It correlates more to poverty and class, racism exacerbates this, and cultures become unequal.

○

CALEB: Are you familiar with the Ted Turner/Robert Olen Butler/Elizabeth Dewberry brouhaha?

DAVID: I don't know who Elizabeth Dewberry is.

CALEB: She was Robert Olen Butler's student in the graduate program at Florida State. Robert Olen Butler was almost twenty years older. Evidently, she was heavy, lost a lot of weight, became a very attractive woman, married Butler, and she's published a few novels. I was talking with Rosemary Daniell at the Faulkner Festival in New Orleans when this attractive couple walked by. The woman shrieked greetings, hugged Rosemary, and then Rosemary introduced me to them: Elizabeth Dewberry and Ted Turner. At first, I didn't know it was him. He's six-three and big, like a linebacker.

DAVID: Why was he at the Faulkner Festival?

CALEB: He was being given some award or other: $10,000 for a billionaire. He was also there to promote his book *Call Me Ted*. And Elizabeth Dewberry had dumped Butler for Ted Turner.

DAVID: What does she look like?

CALEB: She's tall, blonde, svelte. Gorgeous. So Ted and Elizabeth walk off, and Rosemary tells me that evidently during the Dewberry/Butler divorce Robert cc'd an email to his MFA grad students about the breakup. One of the students posted it online and it went viral. This letter got mentioned in the *New York Times*, everywhere. NPR even did something on it.

DAVID: What was in the letter?

CALEB: That Elizabeth had been sexually abused by her grandfather, had an abusive first marriage, and Robert saved her life by his presence, but she never could overcome that he was a successful author and so, according to Robert, the reason they divorced was that she was envious of Robert and his Pulitzer Prize. The letter goes on to say how Elizabeth is now Ted Turner's girlfriend, but that Turner cannot be monogamous. Elizabeth will spend only one week a month with Turner while he rotates women. Elizabeth is attracted to the type of men that abused her, older men, and Ted is like that except he's not abusive. The awards banquet starts and Ted Turner accepts his award and makes a speech.

DAVID: And Robert's there?

CALEB: Near the podium.

DAVID: Oh no.

CALEB: So Ted says a few words about his memoir and then he says, "I've got a flight to catch, so I have to leave. Success is about class. Remember that, Bobby boy." Ted walks out.

DAVID: What did Elizabeth do?

CALEB: She followed Ted out.

DAVID: What's the point?

CALEB: What do you mean, what's the point?

DAVID: It's just another one of your stories.

CALEB: Okay, what do you think the point is?

DAVID: We're all blind as bats.

CALEB: To me, the point is we all suffer. No matter how high you climb, someone will be punching you in the gut.

DAVID: Finally, we're in agreement about something.

○

CALEB: Keep talking. I'll take pictures.

DAVID: I don't think the book will include pictures.

CALEB: It should.

DAVID: Laurie reminded me: if I'm hiking in the woods, pay attention. Otherwise, I might slip. This is a solid walk. Coming back will be easier. I wonder how far we are.

○

CALEB: The fallacy of contradictory authority is when two "experts" contradict each other: Keynes vs. Friedman. Michael Medved is certain that conservative economics fuel the economy. Norman Goldman is certain that conservative economics are harmful.

DAVID: I like Goldman, actually.

CALEB: He's too certain. Both he and Rush are absolutists convinced that their opposition is brainwashed. They field too many calls from sycophants. Medved's not so bad.

DAVID: Does Medved ever marshal a coherent argument?

CALEB: He attacks conservatives, calls Ron Paul a "Losertarian." Medved's a reasonable right-wing talk show host.

DAVID: In what sense?

CALEB: He takes calls from people who disagree, lets them talk. He calls out the fringe, anyone who's a 9/11 Truther or in the Birther movement. He'll ridicule, say, Donald Trump.

DAVID: I do think there were some very odd things about 9/11.

CALEB: Don't tell me you're a Truther.

DAVID: I'm not, but still, Osama's family being allowed to leave the U.S.? Someone gave Bush a memo in early 2001: Osama is going to attack the U.S. with hijacked planes on U.S. soil. Bush thanks the CIA person, says, "You can now consider your ass covered. Thanks. I'll file it under 'W.' "

CALEB: Osama, or Al-Qaeda, had already attacked U.S. embassies in Africa. Newspapers regularly published stuff like "Al-Qaeda promises attacks on U.S. soil." They still do. There probably have been thousands of threats made in 2011 alone that intelligence has picked up, and one of them might happen, and when it does, there will be a conspiracy that "we knew and let it happen."

DAVID: I still think it's amazing how Bush avoided all blame for 9/11, whereas if it had happened on Obama's watch, I don't want to even contemplate what would have happened to him. The left never really attacked Bush, specifically, about 9/11. How'd he escape that?

CALEB: Escape? The left shredded Bush nonstop. They still are.

○

CALEB: The hot tub sounds nice. I'm glad you wanted to do this. I was wondering—soft city slicker?

DAVID: City slicker?

CALEB: You ever change a flat tire?

DAVID: No.

CALEB: I told Terry, "I bet he's never changed a flat tire." She says, "You're not going to ask him that, are you?"

DAVID: You can ask me anything. Laurie does everything. She's Ms. Mechanical.

CALEB: So you're in the middle of nowhere, you get a flat, and she changes it?

DAVID: Well, we've never had that happen, but if it did, we'd call AAA.

CALEB: Ai-yai-yai.

DAVID: Is that horrible? You do construction, and that's the last thing I could do. I married my polar opposite. Laurie's handy and reasonable in ways I'm not. I'm like Bertrand Russell, who didn't know how to boil water. She's incredibly practical. You do all the handyman work?

CALEB: Pretty much. Terry gardens. I dig the holes. Even changing lightbulbs—stuff she could do—she'll have me do.

DAVID: So she's not handy at all?

CALEB: She's self-reliant. If I'm not around, she'll take out the trash, but she works, and these things become my responsibility. She supports the family.

DAVID: I'm like Terry. In a good year, between the UW and all my other teaching gigs and publishing stuff, I make two hundred grand.

CALEB: Damn.

○

DAVID: What would we do if we saw a bear? What are you supposed to do? I forget.

CALEB: It depends: grizzly, black, brown bear. Actually, I don't know—run, punch 'im in the nose, create a diversion, play dead?

DAVID: That would be scary. You play dead, he might come and bite you.

CALEB: Mainly, if it's a mother protecting her cubs: danger.

DAVID: Wow, that's quite a waterfall. It's beautiful. Just beautiful.

CALEB: Funny, how useful that word is in life. Just look and marvel: the lake. We made it!

DAVID: I'm glad we made it.

○

DAVID: Going back, downhill, do you make sure your speed doesn't build up?

CALEB: It's hard on the knees. I climbed Huayna Picchu, almost straight up and down, 800 meters. (I'm "life-dropping," subtly inserting how I went to Machu Picchu.) It's cake compared to K2, but it was hard.

DAVID: How's your Spanish?

CALEB: *No es malo.* It has problems. I'm functional, conversational, but when it's fast I miss a lot.

○

CALEB: There's something appealing in an artist who turns toward contradictions, a troubled and tormented artist who seeks pain. There's mystique, validity, even credibility. You may disagree, but one thing I've observed in your writing is that you seem like you almost wish you had suffered more than you actually have.

DAVID: Then you're a really bad reader and know nothing about my life.

CALEB: Whoa. Whoa. I wasn't saying that as a criticism.

DAVID: You don't think my work turns toward contradictions?

CALEB: Sure, but—

DAVID: You don't think anyone who lives an ordinary life has plenty of trouble and torment to write about? You don't seek out pain; pain—

CALEB: Maybe that's it. Maybe you're interested in ordinary life and I'm interested in extremities of life.

DAVID: I mean, we're all going to die.

CALEB: We all die differently. You're interested in "mortality." I'm interested in murder.

DAVID: We all suffer as human beings.

CALEB: "Pain is mandatory. Suffering is optional."

DAVID: You're quoting my back doctor quoting the—

CALEB: From *Thing About Life*. And then there's Bukowski: "All this writing about pain and suffering is bullshit." For the most part, we're responsible for our own suffering. I realize there are victims of trauma coming from external forces, but for you and me and your students and peers, suffering is different. The widow of Kabul's suffering isn't David Shields's suffering. You say literature saved your life? Really? Really? Your life was in jeopardy? You're not politically or socially oppressed.

DAVID: Wow. That's an incredibly banal and Maoist view of what constitutes suffering. If only the widow of Kabul's suffering counts, why read *Hamlet*? I love the Yeats line that goes, "Why should we honour those that die upon the field of battle? A man may show as reckless a courage in entering into the abyss of himself."

CALEB: Yeats is an artist, he explores his abyss, and then says that takes more courage than facing a bullet?

DAVID: He says as much courage.

CALEB: Whatever.

DAVID: If you take art seriously, it's true.

CALEB: You linger on pain, yours and others. I get the sense that you're exaggerating your own—

DAVID: Agony.

CALEB: Sure, that. Perhaps, when you were younger, your suffering might have been more genuine. Stuttering must have had a tremendous impact. You could function one-on-one, but in groups you must have been terribly introverted. It would have made it difficult to "hang out with the guys."

DAVID: That's right: ever since I gained a little more control of my speech, I've stopped suffering.

○

DAVID: Natalie is insulin-resistant.

CALEB: She's diabetic?

DAVID: Pre-pre-diabetic. I forget if you've ever met her, but she's pretty heavy.

CALEB: Related to the insulin?

DAVID: She doesn't process insulin correctly. Whenever she eats carbs, her body keeps telling her she needs to eat more. She's doing better, though. She's lost thirty pounds in the last year on a very specific regime of medicines, diet, and exercise. We're hoping she keeps seeing progress.

CALEB: When I first started dating Terry, I met her extended family—all happily married, financially secure, and with beautiful children. On the outside everyone seemed perfectly happy. The first time I met Aunt Karen, she said, "I hear you're a writer. Our family must have many stories for you." She married a man who worked hard. At a relatively young age, he retired a millionaire many times over. They have a house in Seattle, one in Leavenworth, one in Palm Desert. Two children, four grandchildren. The picture of the American Dream. Christian, churchgoing, golf, fantastic restaurants, vacations.

So I replied, "Not really. Everyone seems happy, and happiness is pretty boring subject matter."

DAVID: And really fleeting.

CALEB: Ennui sets in. I'd rather be interested and engaged and passionate than happy. Karen smiles and the subject changes. Turns out she stars in her own "good bad novel," as you like to say. Money may not buy happiness, but it alleviates suffering. At about the age of eighteen she started having faints and seizures and was diagnosed as a type 1 diabetic. She went to college and found a husband. When she married Bob, they tried to have children: the first one was a stillbirth and the second was delivered alive but died a few days later, due to doctor error. At the time, doctors used forceps, and it was a—what do you call it?—a feet-first delivery.

DAVID: Breech birth.

CALEB: The doctor crushed the baby's skull.

DAVID: That enough suffering for you?

○

DAVID: You say that I wish I suffered more, that I wish I'd survived the Gulag or something. I'd say I've taken my obsessions—miscommunication or mortality or whatever—and gone as far as I can with them. The goal is to face your own contradictions and blow them up until they become emblematic of human tragedy. It's all anyone does—from Pascal to Maggie Nelson. The Montaigne thing: "Every man contains within himself the entire human condition."

CALEB: Every person has a novel inside.

DAVID: Well, to me, not a novel. I'm not interested in your dream life. I'm interested in your sadness, your self-knowledge. I don't think you have to have survived the Khmer Rouge or come back from Vietnam or served in Churchill's cabinet or been a member of the Mafia. That's history; that's journalism.

CALEB: Does suffering make a person noble or petty?

DAVID: Well, in my case, it's obviously made me incredibly noble.

○

CALEB: Would you agree that life, condensed, has plot?

DAVID: Sure, you're born, you live, you love, you die, but who cares about that story? That's—

CALEB: I—hey, hey, how's it going?

FIRST HIKER: Pretty good. How far to the lake?

CALEB: You got another half hour.

SECOND HIKER: Sweet.

DAVID: It's really beautiful.

FIRST HIKER: After Lake Dorothy, we're going on to Bear Lake.

CALEB: Wow.

DAVID: You guys going to camp?

FIRST HIKER: Two days.

CALEB: Awesome.

DAVID: Nice. Stay warm.

CALEB: That recorded. I'll insert them.

DAVID: Great! Add them for drama. Plot!

○

CALEB: In *How Literature Saved My Life*, you graphically describe an erotic relationship, and how you wore an earring because of her.

DAVID: You're mixing up girls.

CALEB: The last line—

DAVID: I've changed that.

CALEB: But in the last line you say she's a fictional character.

DAVID: I don't say that.

CALEB: Then you say she was quite the tiger in bed, but "there wasn't an ounce of genuine feeling" in her performance.

DAVID: I don't think I say that. I can dig it up later on my laptop.

CALEB: Your point, at least in the draft I read, was how her erotic self was her fake self. That in bed she wasn't "real." But I'd say the opposite. People suppress their erotic selves in life and in bed they become their true selves.

DAVID: I don't know if you do this—google people?

CALEB: Old-girlfriend-google?

DAVID: You can't help be curious. What do they look like now? How have they aged? I googled Jessica Nagel. I found a video of a little interview she did about a novel she wrote. She was a debater in high school, and she's written a couple of novels about debate.

CALEB: Published?

DAVID: Yes, but I haven't read them. All her limits as a person are grafted directly onto her writing. She's deeply shallow—"deeply shallow"? whatever—but that was the very quality, of course, that made her so sexy to me. I last saw her more than twenty-five years ago, but suddenly, watching this interview, my whole body was plugged right back into her: the things about her I was drawn to, the things about her I was put off by, and it was all pretty overwhelming. I just started taking notes. At one time I thought I might write a whole book about her, but that little riff is as far as I got.

CALEB: Writing about sex is just—no matter what—it's just a penis and a vagina. Scientific sex becomes too analytical. Graphic sex becomes porn. In Aleksander Wat's *My Century*, he says sex is the most important thing, yet it's rarely discussed. And then he doesn't say much else about it. We're not able to write freely about it or, better said, we must be very careful.

DAVID: I want to write a book about all that, but I have no idea how to do it without talking about Laurie and she says I better not. I'll write a whole book about Jessica!

CALEB: Perhaps it shows my own insecurity, not as a writer but as a person (I know there's overlap), but I did a lot of kiss-and-tell when I was younger.

DAVID: Who would you tell?

CALEB: The guys. "I went to third base with her . . ."

DAVID: I see. In high school. Well, that would be part of the appeal: you may not have been connecting much with the girls as people, so it was, Okay, I'm going to tell the whole world I'm having sex. Were your friends the same?

CALEB: Lame role models. One of the guys recorded sex with this girl, and it became his brag tape. She's saying stuff like "Oh, fuck me, fuck me."

DAVID: There wasn't videotape?

CALEB: No. Just a cassette recorder underneath the bed. It disgusted me more and more. I overcompensated and went from shallow asshole to preachy asshole. I'm very judgmental of my youth. I was such a creep. I'd be preachy, smothering, and hesitant with girls I wanted to love. Then, when I wanted to fuck, I'd go all Gadarene swine. I'm not sure if I want to write about that part of my life.

DAVID: I would. The more embarrassing and awful, the better.

○

CALEB: I'm a Nazi in the kitchen. I could give you mushrooms to cut.

DAVID: I'll do cleanup.

CALEB: Okay. What should we have, other than salmon and pasta? Green beans?

DAVID: I can't eat green beans: oxalates. Kidney stones. I could have an apple.

CALEB: I'll eat the green beans, and I have red bell peppers. Pasta is pretty filling.

DAVID: Pasta with salmon sounds great. Who are the Huskies playing this weekend—Utah?

CALEB: Sounds right.

DAVID: I find them oddly likable. I like Sarkisian. I like Chris Polk. I like Keith Price. Saturday rolls around and I inevitably find myself running errands and listening to the game on the car radio. What do you think of Hugh Millen on KJR?

CALEB: He's not bad.

DAVID: I think he's amazing. I love how he brings incredibly rococo analysis to bear upon the simplest plays. In a way, life is very simple. What's interesting is the meditation on it.

CALEB: I've tried Brock and Salk, the 710 guys. They're monotonous, say the same thing eight different ways. They're talking about where Jake Locker will go in the draft. Switch channels, turn back to 710 an hour later, and they're talking about where Jake Locker will go in the draft. And they yammer on and on about their personal lives. Once they spent fifteen minutes on how to grill a burger.

DAVID: Is it hyper-macho talk? Isn't that station much more amped up? "Let's be very testosterone-driven men."

CALEB: Perhaps.

DAVID: My favorite thing on KJR is when the Huskies or Seahawks suffer a devastating defeat—all the people calling in, trying to process loss. I'm in heaven.

CALEB: You'd love soccer culture.

DAVID: Through Natalie I've come to know soccer.

CALEB: Kapuściński's *The Soccer War.*

DAVID: Everyone worships that book. I absolutely loved the first twenty pages or so, then it goes completely slack for me. Kitchen-sink is not a writing strategy.

CALEB: There was that Colombian guy, Andrés Escobar, who scored an own goal in the World Cup against the U.S. in LA in 1994. He came home and was murdered in a parking lot. Before the killer fired, he said, "*¡Gracias por el gol en su propia puerta!*" The guy, Humberto Castro Muñoz, was a hit man for a drug lord who lost money gambling on the game. Muñoz went to prison for eleven years. Pretty light sentence, if you ask me.

○

CALEB: My parents were blind to my drug use. Terry's parents aren't so naive.

DAVID: Have you ever tried LSD?

CALEB: Yeah. Have you?

David shakes his head.

CALEB: It creates an illusion of self-knowledge, but—

DAVID: If someone has dropped acid more than, say, a dozen times, I can tell in an instant.

CALEB: It's a laser show: your pixels and rods and cones blend and your mind forms images, hallucinations. Your subconscious creates shapes. It's not like you see an elephant walk out of the forest, but the colors and images merge with your subconscious.

I did LSD and mushrooms, too—always in controlled environments. I quit pot when I was nineteen. I made a couple exceptions after. Last time I smoked pot was at Autzen Stadium, Eugene, Oregon, summer of 1990, at a Grateful Dead concert. And I combined it with LSD. Last time.

DAVID: You're protesting too much.

CALEB: No, really.

DAVID: I've never taken any hallucinogenic drugs.

CALEB: I've done cocaine maybe four or five times in my life.

DAVID: Me, too.

CALEB: It was like strong coffee.

DAVID: I didn't get it.

CALEB: Lasts for twenty minutes at twenty times the price. I had a friend who loved it. I said why? He said I'd never had "good" coke, so he and another guy got this "great" coke. After a couple hours I went to bed. I mean, it was okay, but I didn't get it, either. I woke up in the morning and they were in the same place, loving every minute of it. They went through two hundred dollars' worth in one night and then passed out.

DAVID: Laurie smoked pot in high school, did some coke in college, tried acid a couple of times. You might think I'd be the more—

CALEB: Experimental?

DAVID: Maybe, but she's a little out there in a good way.

CALEB: I did LSD with my two closest friends in high school, Vince and Mark, right after Mark's father died. And then Mark said he never did it.

DAVID: That's what I would have done: pretended to take it and pocket it instead.

○

DAVID: Sometimes, at a hotel, I'll call and say, "Could you send up an extra pillow?" And they'll say, "We're happy to do that, ma'am."

Caleb laughs.

DAVID: I'll get so mad. It's not their fault. But I'm a man. My voice isn't that high, is it?

CALEB: Try speaking lower.

DAVID: If I consciously try, I can get low—pretty *deeeeep*.

CALEB: You're not that low—not soprano, but maybe alto. Certainly not a sexy female voice, mind you. Some women have deep, throaty, sexy voices. You don't. It's a bad woman's voice.

DAVID: Certain times my voice can just deepen. *Deeeeep.* For some reason, on the phone or on tape, it comes out a little higher than it is.

CALEB: Practice *lowwwww*. I think I can hit tenor—*baaaaysss*.

DAVID: Sometimes in class I'll feel very relaxed, very authoritative, and my voice will deepen.

CALEB: One last chance, for the DVR.

DAVID: *Grrreeeeeeoaaarrr!* There. Low enough?

CALEB: Hmm.

DAVID: That's maybe a segue to this: I'm curious how students, including you, processed my stuttering. Was that something students talked about?

CALEB: Not really. Even twenty years ago, it was barely noticeable.

DAVID: That's good to hear. A lot of people say it's no big deal. To me, though, it is.

CALEB: Disfluent speech, to me, is when I try to speak in a foreign language.

DAVID: You tend to stutter?

CALEB: I feel incredibly self-conscious. I fake competence. I can function one-on-one, but not in groups. I ask the speaker to slow down or speak clearly or use simple sentences. When I developed friendships, the friend would learn how to converse and compensate for my weaknesses. I couldn't worry about nailing grammar or pronunciation. I'd just butcher language and make communication the priority. *¿Puedes hablar español?*

DAVID: *No muy bien.*

CALEB: We're going to an all-inclusive, in Mexico, in a couple of months.

DAVID: What does that mean—"all-inclusive"? Hotel, the flight?

CALEB: The price includes hotel, all meals and beverages,

including liquor. It's heaven. Primarily because they have day care.

DAVID: Is there a pool?

CALEB: Adult pools, kid pools, pools where you swim up to a bar. Cafeteria and sit-down dining.

DAVID: All in the same site? And it's all paid for?

CALEB: Except tips. We'll bring a few hundred for tips. Eight days, family of five, direct flight to Cabo: $2,500. I sound like an advertisement, but if you include airport shuttle and tips, it's still a vacation for less than three thousand bucks. . . . Oh, hi. How you doing? Congrats.

FEMALE HIKER: *(with baby in front pack)* Thanks.

CALEB: I did this trail with my wife and newborn. Great hike.

MALE HIKER: Definitely.

CALEB AND DAVID: Take care.

FEMALE HIKER AND MALE HIKER: Bye.

CALEB: In my *Notes of a Sexist Stay-at-Home Father* blog, when I wrote about one of our vacations, I called it "A Supposedly Fun Thing the Powell Family Will Do Again." One of the segments I titled "All-Inclusive Jest." I "rail" against greedy capitalists creating local jobs outside the drug trade.

DAVID: It's not that unusual of an idea to me—the stay-at-home dad—but maybe it could be an idea for a book.

CALEB: Half of all stay-at-home parents (or it seems like half) blog.

DAVID: Terry likes the blog a lot?

CALEB: Sometimes. I make fun of us. Well, her. I think she's soft on punishing the kids. I call her method "Crime and Reward."

DAVID: You're more the disciplinarian?

CALEB: Yes and no. She wants to be the treat-giver, so she gets on me for buying them doughnuts, but then she makes brownies for dinner.

DAVID: I know what you mean. Competition between the parents. Laurie and I do that. Did you want to have a boy?

CALEB: I didn't want a boy bad enough to push for a fourth.

DAVID: I very much wanted a girl. Xenogenesis: the greater likelihood that your offspring will be completely different from you if they are of the opposite sex.

CALEB: You want to stand by the Dorothy Lake sign?

DAVID: I can't believe that was only a mile and a half.

○

Returning on the forest service road.

DAVID: How about if tonight we watch *My Dinner with André*? They worked together at two facing typewriters: "Okay, André, you go off on that long aria about your friends mock-burying you on Long Island. And I'll write about how addicted I am to my electric blanket." I love when Wally has had enough. He pushes back and says, "Surely, life is not like that. Surely, if life is interesting at all, you can find majesty at the local cigar shop as easily as you can in a Peruvian rain forest."

CALEB: Or in the Polish countryside.

DAVID: And then, at the very end, Wally is talking about how all the streets look magical, and André is saying, Yes, I really love my wife and kids. There's a very subtle changing of the guard. Which I think is crucial to this genre. *Sideways, My Dinner with André, The Trip*: at the end the characters switch roles in a way that feels credible. Something we should obviously aim for. I thought we did that a little as we were arguing about Bush.

CALEB: That's all great, but I don't know if I'm willing to flip, or make a gesture, because of "art." I don't want to be David Lipsky to your David Foster Wallace.

○

CALEB: In *Bowling for Columbine,* Michael Moore goes across Lake Michigan to Toronto, knocking on doors and checking to see if they're locked. Moore would say, "I'm sorry, I'm just filming a movie, and I'm checking to see why Canadians don't lock their doors." Brian Fawcett opened one of the doors.

DAVID: Moore just happened to be in Fawcett's neighborhood?

CALEB: Yup. I liked the movie and I'm against gun ownership, but Moore's like Oliver Stone in that, whether you agree or not, it's propaganda and straw-man arguments.

DAVID: But you're obviously capable of a certain amount of political posturing yourself. I actually like Michael Moore and I can sort of tolerate Oliver Stone.

CALEB: Today's artists too often adopt the same liberal ideologies. I'm disillusioned with the left.

DAVID: In what areas are you moving away from the left?

CALEB: Too often, I just find the left absolutist and delusional.

DAVID: Any particular issues you find the left wrong on?

CALEB: Unions. The film *Waiting for "Superman"* does a good job on how unions protect incompetent public school teachers. In Chicago the union is so strong they put three waste-disposal employees on every truck. In every other municipality in the U.S., each truck has two employees. Rahm Emanuel has been trying to clean up Richard Daley's mess, and the union won't let him fire anyone. Go to South Korea or Taiwan or Thailand: you got workers on the job twelve hours a day, six days a week. In these places, you get hurt on the job and you're fucked. Let's bring in unions. But the left has this "union: good/capitalism: bad" shtick.

DAVID: I'm detecting NewsCorp's influence.

CALEB: The director of *Waiting for "Superman"* is a big Obama supporter. It's the left policing the left. We need more of that.

○

DAVID: I like Chomsky's view that the United States is the freest country on earth, but that it's still incredibly flawed. Even if he often overshoots the mark, he's still a valuable voice.

CALEB: I guess you see the obvious. Chomsky is half wrong. And in politics or religion "half wrong" equals "all wrong." The U.S. needs criticism, but it's got to come from a free agent, not Chomsky. He's become an intellectual demagogue.

DAVID: I'd say he's pure demagogue. I just like how carefully and quietly and pseudo-respectfully he speaks, as if he's saying very normative things.

CALEB: My problem with him is he misuses his authority. He's still the same guy who misread Cambodia, citing Western propaganda that only 8,000 people died. Chomsky's misreading directly influenced how leftist intellectuals approached Cambodia. Chomsky never adequately, as you like to say, "turns the arrow back upon himself." And he's gotten progressively worse. After they killed Osama, Chomsky said, "Bin Laden's 'confession' is like my confession that I won the Boston Marathon." Talk about a perpendicular analogy. In 1967 Chomsky wrote "The Responsibility of Intellectuals." He has failed to answer his own call.

DAVID: I'm mainly fascinated by him as a presence.

CALEB: "A presence"? That's it?

DAVID: Listen, Caleb. You've done more things out in the world than I have, but I've figured out how to write about it in my own voice. I know how to place a jar in Tennessee. It's all I know how to do, but that, to me, is everything.

CALEB: A jar in Tennessee?

DAVID: Wallace Stevens.

CALEB: It's not everything.

DAVID: To me, it is.

CALEB: If that's all you have, it's nothing.

DAVID: That's because you don't have it.

CALEB: That's a pretty dickish thing to say, don't you think?

DAVID: You're right. I apologize. Let's agree to disagree. Let's take a break.

○

CALEB: At the Philoctetes Center panel, you, Rick Moody, and John Cameron Mitchell couldn't get a word in because DJ Spooky just kept talking about nothing, saying shit like "The bizarre right-wing rescripting of reality is exactly what Hitler was doing: creating a notion of fear and terror as a narrative frame." The moderator put a stop to it with an interjection about Freud and the vagina. Moody says, "Excellent point." And they successfully change the topic.

DAVID: I was supposed to be the moderator of the discussion, but—

CALEB: It was a lively conversation.

DAVID: I'd never met Paul Miller—that's DJ Spooky's real name, as you probably know—and he was a last-minute replacement for someone else. He's obviously smart and he talks a good game and he's—

CALEB: He's no dumb-dumb, but he needs someone to tell him to shut up.

DAVID: I should have just said, "Paul, thanks, but let's let other people jump in." It was a conscious decision on my part: the whole room would have gone cold. If Rick Moody were talking too much, I would have said, "Rick, c'mon, give it a rest. You're talking up a storm."

CALEB: An ice storm.

DAVID: Ha ha.

CALEB: But you wouldn't say anything to Spooky?

DAVID: Would you have?

CALEB: I'd like to think so.

DAVID: Endless blathering and name-dropping and never really saying anything. I wish I'd called him on it. I didn't.

CALEB: I name-drop, I life-drop, I've done this, I've done that, but there's a time and place.

DAVID: Because he's black, I just didn't feel comfortable shutting him down.

CALEB: Speaking of which, what's this about you listening to hip-hop? I just can't see David Shields thundering down the road listening to N.W.A.—you know, Niggaz with Attitude.

DAVID: You don't think I know who N.W.A. are!? You have a completely one-dimensional view of me. I like hip-hop as it enters my ears through my friend Michael and through Natalie. I don't pretend to seek it out.

◌

In the kitchen.

CALEB: Beer?

DAVID: Sure. *(sound of beer bottle opening)* Amazing. That's an experienced beer drinker. I've never seen that.

CALEB: Terry's not a fan of the wedding-ring bottle opener.

DAVID: Why not?

CALEB: She thinks it'll scratch up the ring. I say it's a symbol of devotion. Beer. Wife. Love.

○

CALEB: What'd I do with the black pepper? You want some?
DAVID: That's plenty. Thanks a lot. This sauce is very good. It's really delicious.
CALEB: Thanks.

○

CALEB: In *Elizabeth Costello,* Coetzee alludes to our treating animals similarly to the way Nazis treated Jews.
DAVID: I'm not a vegetarian, but I wish I had the willpower. Coetzee says about *Eating Animals,* "Anyone who, after reading Foer's book, continues to consume factory farm products must be without a heart, or impervious to reason, or both."
CALEB: Ugh.
DAVID: If you watch a documentary like—
CALEB: It's a bunch—
DAVID: If you watch how chickens are slaughtered, it should make you feel guilty. Don't you think it's cruel how animals are slaughtered, and yet we do it for our own convenience?

Do you not think there's a legitimate case to be made for vegetarianism?

CALEB: We're omnivores. Animals suffer. That's what they do. They eat one another, battle the elements, starve. They're not cognizant the way we are. In a rich, liberal, educated society it's easy to be a "moral vegetarian," but in Africa and Southeast Asia they don't eat animals because they can't afford to. Kids suffer mineral and iron and vitamin deficiency. And the brain can't develop without nutrients that meats provide. Pregnant mothers need meat, eggs, milk to help nourish their fetus, so poor people die or grow up malnourished as relatively prosperous vegetarians eat tofu and watercress and hijiki and organic tempeh and then tsk-tsk about meat being "murder."

DAVID: Do you try to eat from organic farms?

CALEB: Terry is nuts about it; so is my dad. We eat free-range chicken, organic everything. All the vegetables we're eating tonight are locally produced. We avoid red meat because it's unhealthy.

○

CALEB: When it comes to food, guns, abortion, I'm pro-choice. Smoking: it's your choice. I'm anti-cigarettes but pro-choice. Nobody's pro-abortion.

DAVID: I think the pro-abortion side believes it can't keep compromising. The so-called pro-life movement's ultimate goal is to ban abortion completely.

CALEB: There are those who fear if we ban assault rifles, we're going to ban hunting.

DAVID: I tend to buy the pro-choice argument and I tend not to buy the pro-gun movement.

CALEB: Guns we agree on, but no one's trying to ban them. The pro-choice, anti-death-penalty, moral vegetarian, though— what is such a person saying? That a fetus has less value than a convicted criminal or a chicken? Terry's friend Jenny and her husband stopped eating meat for moral reasons. Then Jenny had an abortion while she was going to nursing school. A couple summers ago we had a barbecue, and before they could grill their vegetables, they take a wire brush and start cleaning the grill so meat by-products won't pollute their vegetables. I tell Terry, "Chicken has more value than a human fetus?"

DAVID: You have a distant, detached perspective on human foibles. You're good at that, I think. You're very logical.

CALEB: Of course I didn't say anything. Jenny felt horrible, though. It messed with her mind. When she told her mother about the abortion, rather than offer consolation, she went ballistic, accusing Jenny of "aborting my grandchild." Now they don't talk. And I think Jenny regrets her choice. So there's that.

○

CALEB: Tell me the Coetzee blurb story. Every time I asked before, you were completely evasive.

DAVID: I love *Elizabeth Costello* as much as any book published in the last ten years.

CALEB: A very boring book.

DAVID: You're joking, right?

CALEB: Not at all.

DAVID: I'd go to the mat for that book. I handwrote Coetzee a fan letter and tried to articulate what I like so much about it—basically, that every chapter is an evisceration of the moral/aesthetic stance of one of his previous books, and the book as a whole is an attempt to try to figure out what if anything in life is worthwhile. At the end, he can affirm only the belling of frogs in mud: sheer animal survival. It's an incredibly serious and great book. I sent him the letter; he liked what I said. This is all by snail mail.

CALEB: Snail mail? Australia?

DAVID: I didn't have his email.

CALEB: Your penmanship is horrible.

DAVID: Just let me—

CALEB: Moo.

DAVID: After a few exchanges, I described *Reality Hunger* and asked him if he'd be willing to read a tape-bound manuscript. To my surprise, he said yes.

CALEB: Get to the point.

DAVID: Basically, what happened is he wrote a blurb, I conflated it with another email he'd written to me, and asked him if it was okay to merge the official blurb with his unofficial blurb. I didn't think it was that big of a deal.

CALEB: *(laughing)* He did.

DAVID: I can't count how many times people have done that with my emails, but he said, "No, it's not okay. Please use only the official blurb." I said, "Absolutely. Of course. No problem."

CALEB: Only, there was a problem.

DAVID: A few weeks earlier I'd sent the blurb to my editors in the U.S. and UK and a few other people. As soon as I got Coetzee's request, I made the correction, but then Zadie Smith wrote a review in the *Guardian* months before the book came out, and she quoted the fuller, wrong, unofficial blurb. The moment I saw that on the web, I'm like, What the fuck!?

CALEB: For the record, the sesquipedalian David Shields just said, "I'm like, What the fuck!?"

DAVID: First of all, I wasn't thrilled with her take on the book, and second of all—I'm going to get an apple. Hold on.

David gets an apple, takes a bite. Caleb gets a beer, takes a drink.

Second of all, the moment I saw that Coetzee quote, my heart just fell out of my rib cage.

Caleb laughs.

DAVID: I wrote to him immediately, "One of the red-letter days of my life was when I got the statement from you that you liked my book. You're one of the half-dozen writers I most admire in the world. It's entirely my fault. I sincerely apologize. I promise to make sure only the correct quote gets used going forward." And that's the last I ever heard from him. From then on it was Coetzee's agent, who said no publisher can use the quote. Coetzee wrote a letter to the *Guardian*, which had to take the review down. Zadie Smith couldn't republish the essay.

CALEB: The quotes are public. How many galleys exist?

DAVID: Maybe four hundred.

CALEB: Really? That makes the galleys collectors' items. If someone offered me a thousand bucks for my copy, I wouldn't sell it.

DAVID: Did I do anything wrong, exactly?

CALEB: You kind of did.

DAVID: Here's a writer I really admire and I—

CALEB: I should blog it.

DAVID: Don't do that.

CALEB: Why not? Fair use.

DAVID: Well, there's a legal stricture.

CALEB: Who would be liable—you or me?

DAVID: I doubt it'd be you.

CALEB: I won't do it, then.

DAVID: For this relief, much thanks.

○

CALEB: I was disappointed when you refused to offer whole-hearted praise of my rape novel.

DAVID: That was an awkward situation.

CALEB: How could it have hurt you? You wrote, more or less, "I've just written *Reality Hunger,* a manifesto partly in dispraise of traditional novels, so I probably shouldn't blurb traditional novels."

DAVID: What happened in the meantime was the Coetzee mess. I was thinking, Coetzee's acting rather high-handed toward me. I'm not going to act high-handed toward Caleb.

CALEB: I was pissed. Then I got your permission.

DAVID: What'd I say?

CALEB: You said not to call your former teacher names, and that I could use any praise you'd written. My novel didn't deserve a glowing blurb, but still—

DAVID: What did you call me, do you remember?

CALEB: I said, "You're really a dork."

DAVID: Third-grade stuff.

CALEB: You immediately responded with "What do you mean?" Then, a few minutes later, you wrote, "You're wildly overreacting."

DAVID: I think that's true, don't you?

CALEB: Probably.

DAVID: I forget what I said.

CALEB: You'd written about my book, "Your book is gorgeously written and the ending is quite powerful, but unfortunately I can't blurb it because I have a book coming out that—"

DAVID: That makes sense, to me, actually; after *Reality Hunger*—

CALEB: Fair enough.

DAVID: Well, I liked your novel.

CALEB: Apparently not enough.

○

DAVID: Thanks. That was really good. I'm used to Laurie's cooking and that was right up there. Let me do the dishes.

CALEB: We can use the dishwasher. I need to beer up. (*goes to get a beer*)

○

DAVID: I think it's a fascinating wrestling match between you and me on *Elizabeth Costello*. Your take is: Here is an Afghani widow, and there is Coetzee worrying about his legacy, but the book is not "Woe is me—I'm a misunderstood Nobel Prize winner." Coetzee is saying, "I'm trying to stay alive as a writer and not be buried under the avalanche of applause. I'm now a man in my mid-sixties. I want to ask the ultimate question."

CALEB: What's the ultimate question?

DAVID: What, in life, can I actually affirm? Not pseudo-affirm, but what do I actually believe in? And after all these great chapters about animal rights, civil rights, political activism, art, love, friendship, I believe in the belling of—

CALEB: What you said earlier.

DAVID: Your critique of Coetzee is, to me, the same as your critique of Wallace: "Enough whining—give me the agony of the world without all of your precious consciousness between me and the world." But to me, that's what art is: human consciousness.

CALEB: "Consider the Lobster," "Shipping Out"—they're engaging, but my problem with Wallace is I don't think the reader should have to work that hard. He vacillates between esoteric and overwritten.

DAVID: You think he brandishes his authority too much?

CALEB: He is—he was—a cool guy.

DAVID: I would say he was probably the least cool guy in the history of the planet.

CALEB: You can tell that spending time with him probably was a kick. He needed someone, though, to pull him aside, inspire him, make him not feel so lonely. An editor. A lover.

DAVID: I think if he had had that, he wouldn't have become anything like the much-loved writer he was. His whole project was nothing more or less than trying to convey and articulate and embody how strange it felt to be alive, especially to think, now—the pleasures and burdens of being conscious. So every footnote, every neologism, every weird mix of highfalutin diction and pop jargon, every overuse of "w/r/t" or "like" as a filler, every qualifying parenthesis—the goal was to try to talk in a new way about what it felt like to be alive at ground level right now.

CALEB: I'd be Mr. Interrupting Cow. Maybe his IQ goes over my head.

DAVID: You're an extremely intelligent person.

CALEB: I have limits. I don't suffer from low self-esteem, but I know I'm clueless. I just don't make this my front-and-center.

DAVID: Who cares what his IQ was? Wallace figured out how to sound smart on the page. He said that pretty much everyone at Pomona College, where he taught, had higher SAT scores than he did. I studied Latin in high school and college and graduate school, and he constantly misuses it.

CALEB: Is he aware of that?

DAVID: No, he's just misusing it. And that helps me understand him as a vulnerable person who tried very hard to sound incredibly smart, but here's an area I happen to know well, and he's often hilariously wrong. The point being that he wasn't necessarily a "genius," whatever that means. It's that he found a way to sound really smart and funny on the page.

CALEB: Interesting. Maybe his IQ goes beneath my head.

DAVID: Exactly. He was stupid enough to commit suicide.

CALEB: I've got two suicidal friends: one was manic-depressive/bipolar, and the other had fits of depression, but now they're on medication.

DAVID: That was Wallace.

CALEB: Some people—their synapses don't connect.

DAVID: It's pure biochemistry, isn't it? As young as fourteen or fifteen, Wallace was imagining that he had an axe sticking out of his forehead. He always felt there was a glass wall between himself and the world and was on Nardil for most of his life. Then he had that great job at Pomona, was happily married, was hoping to have a child, and he said, "I want to take this happiness to the next level." And he went off Nardil. Big mistake: he spiraled into severe depression. What happens, sometimes, with these meds, is that when you try to use them again, you can't. They've lost their kick for you. When he tried to get back on it, it wasn't the same. He tried everything, including electroshock, which my father submitted himself to every few years the last half of his life.

CALEB: Did you know him—Wallace?

DAVID: Slightly.

CALEB: I should retract some of what I said. I feel cruel.

DAVID: Not at all.

◦

CALEB: This song is called "James Wood Is a Dinosaur." *(strums a guitar chord and sings, à la Paul Shaffer)* James Wood is a dinosaur. *(strums a chord progression)* James Wood don't know the score. *(plays loudly, then softly)* James Wood makes David Shields snore.

DAVID: Stick to learning foreign languages.

CALEB: *(to DVR)* It's now 9:37 p.m., Friday, September 30th.

DAVID: What's my problem with James Wood? He's confused literature with religion.

CALEB: *(sings)* Literature with religion!

DAVID: His, you know, his fuddy-duddyness.

CALEB: *(sings)* His fuddy-duddyness!

DAVID: I've read his two collections of reviews. I've read *How Fiction Works*, which is incredibly banal. I've actually read his novel about God, which is even worse.

CALEB: *(lightly strums)* I haven't. Just the occasional piece in the *New Yorker*.

DAVID: He fascinates me as a case or type. His father was an Anglican priest, and Wood was raised to also become a man of the cloth. He left the church to become a literary critic, but he never left—that old story. In 2011, he's still clinging to the "great tradition." Every contemporary work is judged according to how well it measures up to *Madame Bovary*.

Caleb laughs.

DAVID: He's thought to be the gold standard for people who do book reports, when what he is is a sea captain for nineteenth-century novels. He is, to me, one lost human, movingly so, but it's really important to push back against his rearguard action.

○

DAVID: In *My Dinner with André,* Wally feels compelled to have dinner with André because André's in the throes of a meltdown. I wonder, with Caleb and David, if we can concoct something similar. Maybe Caleb has a manuscript he wants me to read. Or I want him to interview me about *How Literature Saved My Life.* Or he's mad that I didn't blurb his manuscript. Or he needs a recommendation to apply to graduate school.

CALEB: Too staged.

DAVID: Just the tiniest thing at the beginning . . .

CALEB: I don't know.

DAVID: I'm just throwing it out there.

CALEB: Well, if we're going to imitate *My Dinner with André,* we could start with me walking to meet you at your UW office. Voice-over: "Hmm, David Shields asked me if I'd be interested in collaborating on a book. Why? Is this some cruel joke? I thought he hated me."

DAVID: Or a possible trigger could be that David seeks Caleb out because David has become a bit of a pamphleteer, a blabberer about art and culture, which bores him greatly, and he doesn't want to keep doing this. And yet he can't exactly come up with anything else to do. He fears he may have few if any arrows left in his quiver. He needs something, someone, to shake him up. He wants an opponent, and he recalls Caleb as an aggressive—

CALEB: You've used "combative" and "contentious."

DAVID: You're one of the most confrontational people I know.

CALEB: You called me "hostile."

DAVID: I did.

CALEB: I take that as a compliment. And a complement. Ba-boom! We're somewhat friendly, though.

DAVID: You've always been willing to take me on, and yet we have a shared enough aesthetic that we don't not have anything to talk about. Like André and Wally . . .

CALEB: Like André, I can disappear. I told Terry, before we got married, that I'm the sort of guy who can disappear for three months and still be happy in a marriage. When she confirmed a healthy pregnancy, I went back to Asia. That was part of our informal prenuptial, but even then, she didn't understand how I could do this. Her mother, especially, didn't: "Your wife's pregnant and you're going to Taiwan?" André leaves his wife and family, too.

DAVID: You have huge wanderlust.

CALEB: I proposed and went to Taiwan for six months. We met in Hong Kong for a week, but she did all the marriage plans. Her family and mine thought that was weird. I come home from Asia, we get married, and then honeymoon in

Belize and Guatemala. At our wedding, her father makes a toast and says Terry and I are so similar—both of us have wanderlust. He says, "Caleb has traveled all around the world. And when my daughter's employer asked if she'd be willing to relocate to Maryland, Terry went." Ever since, I tease my wife about the great adventure of Maryland.

DAVID: She never worked in Asia?

CALEB: No.

DAVID: Maybe she's like André's wife.

CALEB: André doesn't evoke his wife.

DAVID: Sure he does. I have a very specific sense of her.

CALEB: We know hardly anything about her. Trivia: she's sitting in the bar as an extra.

○

DAVID: (talking into the DVR with Caleb out of the room) Wally and André cartoonize themselves in order to make the contrast starker: Quixote tilting at windmills; Sancho Panza, quotidian man. And I think Caleb and I should be willing—in our conversations per se and/or in our edits of our conversations—to slightly exaggerate our positions. Not lie or pretend, but I seriously doubt André is as high-church as he comes across, and I know Wallace Shawn is much more sophisticated than the nudnik he presents himself as being. In the same way, Caleb and I ought to be willing to do the same thing in the service of a work of art whose main debate topic is, let's face it, life vs. art.

I've never lived abroad for more than four months. Caleb has lived abroad for maybe a quarter of his life, and yet, of course, he's the stay-at-home dad. I like that there are all these contradictions; otherwise, the whole thing would be a one-line joke about writing books compared to changing diapers. I'm not sure how we'll carve out our personalities. I don't have enough distance on myself to know precisely *what* my personality is. If I even have one. Ha ha. In *Although Of Course*, DFW is art; Lipsky is very crass commerce. In *Sideways*, Giamatti is Anxious Writer; Haden Church is We Pass This Way But Once. Perhaps that shows the limit of these works. Caleb and I ought to strive to push beyond these name tags.

CALEB: *(returning to the room)* There's also *Rosencrantz and Guildenstern*.

DAVID: Christ, I love that play so much.

CALEB: *Waiting for Godot*.

DAVID: Obviously, you can go all the way back to Plato's dialogues with Socrates. It's an ancient form: two white guys bullshitting. I also like the idea of us asking ourselves, Why are we even doing this? Why aren't we home with our wives and children? I even like the idea of us talking about Lipsky/Wallace, *Sideways*, *The Trip*. I wonder if it would be too weird for us to consciously discuss them.

CALEB: We need comedy, like in *Sideways* when Thomas Haden Church is tasting wine and Paul Giamatti discovers he's chewing gum.

DAVID: That was hilarious.

CALEB: Terry thinks that's me, Haden Church.

DAVID: How so?

CALEB: She thinks I'm unsophisticated.

DAVID: Oh, is she so sophisticated herself?

CALEB: She knows all the rules and etiquette of dining, hosting, being a guest, furniture placement. With pillows the stems must point downward; and with flowers, they must point upward.

DAVID: I have no idea what that even means.

CALEB: Floral patterns on the pillows. And the difference between Malbec and Cabernet and Merlot. Once, I handed her a thin-stemmed glass instead of wide-mouthed, and she says, "Caleb, thanks, but wrong glass. The curves allow the essence of the wine to circulate."

DAVID: Laurie's a little like that. Her father grew up in a house with a maid and a cook. Doesn't Terry acknowledge that you're sophisticated when it comes to thinking about—

CALEB: I've grown increasingly stupid the longer we've been together. She thinks I've undersold myself, that I could have been a doctor, lawyer, etc. She can't understand my motivation, or lack thereof—how is it I've never made more than $22,000 a year?

DAVID: How did you make that, from teaching English?

CALEB: Construction. I never made much teaching English. There were benefits—housing, usually. In Brazil I made $500 a month, and when I worked in the UAE I made the most.

DAVID: Let's watch the movie.

CALEB: Let me get a beer.

○

DAVID: *(alone again, speaking into the DVR)* Another thing I love about Wally and André is their self-mockery. They're really clued in to their own ridiculousness. They often say, "I'm an idiot," which is central to my liking anyone. I do think that Caleb and I should do that. Or, really, just Caleb. Why would I ever have to say that? I've never done anything idiotic.

I hope Caleb and I wind up speaking about the same amount of time, though I like the way Wally stays so long in the background, just waiting to pounce. He's aggressive in his passivity; he's just biding time. The whole movie turns on Wally finally saying, "Do you want to know what I think about all this?" And then he gives his monologue, which to my way of thinking gently demolishes André. Or at least André's argument.

I don't know if I'll find the moment, but I want there to be a place where I say, "Well, thanks, Caleb, for all those amazing stories about Tibet and Istanbul and Cuernavaca. I'm really enjoying listening to all these tall tales, but, you know, here's what I really think. I think you're totally wrong."

CALEB: I'm back.

○

Wally: (voice-over narration) . . . [André had] been seized by a fit of ungovernable crying when the character played by Ingrid Bergman had said, "I could always live in my art, but never in my life" . . .

I THINK YOU'RE TOTALLY WRONG

DAVID: That, to me, is the most important line of the movie.

CALEB: Why?

DAVID: Perhaps not most important. The line I identify with the most.

CALEB: There's a difference?

André: . . . a kind of SS totalitarian sentimentality in there somewhere . . . that love of, um—well, that masculine love of a certain kind of oily muscle. You know what I mean?

DAVID: The specter of the Holocaust haunts the film. It's very intentional. André returns to it over and over again. He was born in France in 1934. Both of them are completely assimilated Jews.

André: . . . but since I've come back home I've just been finding the world we're living in more and more upsetting . . . and I saw this woman who looked as bad as any survivor of Auschwitz or Dachau . . .

· · ·

André: Have you read Martin Buber's book On Hasidism?

Wally: No.

André: Well, here's a view of life.

DAVID: Can you pause while I go to the bathroom? Caleb?

Caleb is snoring.

DAVID: Caleb?

CALEB: Uhh?

DAVID: Pause.

CALEB: Okay, sorry.

DAVID: No problem.

Wally: I mean, people used to treat me—I mean, uh, you know, if I would go to a party of professional or literary people—I mean, I was just treated, uh, in the nicest sense of the word, uh, like a dog. . . . Let's face it. I mean, there's a whole enormous world out there that I just don't ever think about. I certainly don't take responsibility for how I've lived in that world. I mean, you know, if I were actually to sort of confront the fact that I'm sort of sharing this stage with-with-with this starving person in Africa somewhere, well, I wouldn't feel so great about myself. So naturally I just—I just blot all these people right out of my perception. So, of course—of course, I'm ignoring a whole section of the real world. . . .

CALEB: Every artist thinks about this. Or should.

DAVID: I.e., it's what your work is about, so you think it's the sine qua non of literary art. I'd say if in your work you consciously try to think about the world like this, you're doomed to fail.

Wally: . . . But frankly, you know, when I write a play, in a way one of the things I guess I think I'm trying to do is trying to bring myself up against some little bits of reality and I'm trying to share that, uh, with an audience. I mean—I mean, of course we all know, uh, the theater is, uh, in terrible shape today. I mean, uh—I mean, at least a few years ago people who really cared about the theater used to say, "The theater is dead." And now everybody's redefined the theater in such a trivial way that, I mean—I mean, God. I know people who are involved with the theater who go to see things now that—I mean, a few years ago these same people would have just been embarrassed to have even seen some of these plays.

DAVID: Same with books.

André: It may very well be that ten years from now people will pay $10,000 in cash to be castrated just in order to be affected by something.

CALEB: André is insane.
DAVID: What do you think *Fight Club* was about?

André: When I was at Findhorn, I met this extraordinary English tree expert . . . He said, "I think that New York is the new model for the new concentration camp where the camp has been built by the inmates themselves." . . . We really feel like Jews in Germany in the late '30s . . . I think it's quite possible that the 1960s represented the last burst of the human being before he was extinguished and that this is the beginning of the rest of the future now, and that from now on there'll simply be all these robots walking around, feeling nothing, thinking nothing.

CALEB: André's beginning to sound like DJ Spooky.
DAVID: Here's where it turns. Just watch.

Wally: Do you want to know my actual response to all this? Do you want to hear my actual response?

DAY 2

DAVID: Acch. So beautiful. I love this so much.

Wally: I mean, I just—I just don't know how anybody could enjoy anything more than I enjoy, uh, reading Charlton Heston's auto-biography or, uh, you know, uh, getting up in the morning and having the cup of cold coffee that's been waiting for me all night still there for me to drink in the morning and no cockroach or fly has—has died in it overnight. I mean, I'm just so thrilled when I get up and I see that coffee there, just the way I wanted it. I mean, I just can't imagine how anybody could enjoy something else any more than that. I mean, I mean, obviously, if the cockroach—if there is a dead cockroach in it, well, then I just have a feeling of disappointment, and I'm sad. But I mean, I—I just—I just don't think I feel the need for anything more than all this.

CALEB: Wally sure likes to say "I mean" a lot.

André: . . . just as the Nazi demons that were released in the '30s . . .
Wally: . . . Heidegger said that, uh, if you were to experience your own being to the full you'd be experiencing the decay of that being toward death as a part of your experience . . .

· · ·

André: What does that mean—a "wife," a "husband," a "son"? A baby holds your hands and then suddenly there's this huge man lifting you off the ground and then he's gone. Where's that son?

· · ·

Wally: (voice-over narration) . . . When I finally came in, Debbie was home from work and I told her everything about my dinner with André.

DAVID: That gorgeous Erik Satie piano as the camera pans the stores Wally went to as a child—it's hard to think of a more perfect ending to anything.

In *Sideways,* Haden Church asks Giamatti why he wasn't hurt in the car accident they pretended to have. Giamatti says, "I was wearing a seatbelt." And Haden Church says, "Right." You realize that Giamatti's more of a survivor, finally, than Haden Church is. Haden Church bluffs better, that's all.

CALEB: He's a hedonist who realizes—or doesn't—his own faults.

DAVID: Well, good night. Thanks for dinner. Tomorrow I'd love to go into Skykomish, if that's cool. I'll treat for breakfast. Lunch, if we get up late.

CALEB: Wow, it's past midnight. It's almost one.

DAVID: We started close to ten, and we stopped to make notes.

CALEB: I was trying to fight sleep.

DAVID: You slept for an hour, easily.

CALEB: I missed that much?

DAVID: You snored through all the major epiphanies.

CALEB: I thought I missed maybe five minutes.

DAVID: You were out cold. See you tomorrow.

DAY 3

DAVID: I think it's a very good story, but if I were you, I'd rework a couple of things. First, you need to evoke Eliza better. You write, "Yes, she has sexual attributes, but why shall I tell you about them?" This probably sounds like conventional creative writing advice, but the whole story pivots on the narrator trying to get over Eliza, so I would do something to make the reader feel that ache. Then there's this long section where you're endlessly playing out the confusion surrounding her transvestitism, but we already know this from the opening.

CALEB: But the narrator doesn't.

DAVID: But we do. How stupid can the narrator be?

CALEB: He knows afterward.

DAVID: Of course. It starts to feel like—what was that movie?

CALEB: *The Crying Game.*

DAVID: It feels like we're watching *The Crying Game* for the fifth time. What's so interesting about you to me, and what's so different to me about you, is that even if it's a bit of a fiction, you pride yourself on "I'm a man of experience and adventure. I've done this and I've done that. I've traveled here and I've traveled there. I know this person. I know that person."

Whereas me, I'm so much not that person. I don't pretend to be street-smart. I've read books. I've written books. I'm not a complete idiot, I hope, when it comes to that other stuff.

CALEB: What other stuff?

DAVID: Everything that isn't in books. Life, I guess. The story gets to something very deep about you or one version about you. It's a fascinating decision where the guy says, more or less, "You know, our charge on earth is to experience everything," so he calls himself out and makes a potentially suicidal choice. He plans to prove his manhood to himself by, er, fucking this guy. I really want more about this guy who circumlocutes himself into such a pretzel of logic that he convinces himself, suicidally or potentially suicidally, to have sex with someone because the gay guy calls out the narrator's masculinity over being willing to have more experience. That's the story. And that's you. From the age of twenty-six to thirty-four you roamed all over the map. You tried to resist the blandishments of ordinary life. You're understandably and justifiably—

CALEB: Your observations are valid. You've hit flaws. To me, the story is about homophobia and how far a gay-friendly person might go. I wanted to layer in, as you would say, this sexual culture that accepts transvestites: in Polynesia, when a family has too many boys, they raise the youngest as a girl. So I first wrote about two guys, the narrator and his friend. They meet two transvestites, go to this beach, the narrator pulls at the bra, and then, in shock, shouts to his friend, "Stop!" The friend says, "Why? I'm getting my dick sucked! This better be important." The narrator says,

"These girls have dicks!" The friend screams, "Aaaaaah!" And the two friends run into the night back to the hostel.

DAVID: This happened to you?

CALEB: I'll tell you eventually.

DAVID: Well, now I'm obviously—

CALEB: The story goes on. The next day the Australian guy tells his two friends about the culture. One friend is pissed, gets drunk and violent: "These fags—I want revenge!" My narrator says, "Well, it's no big deal, it's our secret, but hey, that's their culture. What if you were dressed like a woman from infancy?" The two guys go out that night, get drunk, the friend asks a transvestite to dance, and then goes off with the transvestite. The narrator follows, discovers his friend beating the hell out of the transvestite, and then pulls him off.

DAVID: And these transvestites were prostitutes.

CALEB: Probably. I also wrote another version of the story and focused only on me.

DAVID: That's the one I'd be more interested in.

CALEB: In this second draft I receive oral sex, but I don't know it's really a guy, and then I step back. I want to bring in the culture, anthropology, literary, historical references.

DAVID: You probably need to make it much longer.

CALEB: Have you ever been hit on by a gay man?

DAVID: Sure.

CALEB: What happened?

DAVID: I said no thanks.

CALEB: I have a gay friend, Matt. One day I asked him, "Have you ever had sex with a woman?" And he says, "Yeah, a few times." "How many?" He says, "Three." I say, "How was it?" He says, "Not bad. Like eating an ice cream flavor you're not crazy about. It's better than no dessert but doesn't really satisfy." Many gay people try heterosexual sex, but not the opposite.

To me, it's a very complex story: in 3,000 words I weave Maugham's closet homosexuality with his unhappy marriage and love of catamites and his short story "Rain," Madonna's bisexual eroticism, Gauguin, Margaret Mead, the Kinsey Scale, Oedipus, Oscar Wilde.

DAVID: But these threads are never really woven into a single—

CALEB: I think to write this as fiction is a greater challenge.

DAVID: No it's not, but either way, you need to show more of the narrator's Puritanism. I think the story has to be "Beast in the Jungle" or *The Good Soldier,* in which the protagonist is far more repressed than he realizes. It should be interesting when he says, "Eliza has erotic qualities, but I can't go into it." Red flag!

CALEB: There's no—

DAVID: Wait. Let me finish. You can have the narrator always protesting too much, and the reader may find him interestingly repressed; that could be a very powerful story, a little like Glenway Wescott's novella *Pilgrim Hawk.* Or you could flip it into an essay or essaylike story in which the author-narrator really investigates these ideas and, under the pressure of Maugham and Wilde and Madonna, thinks that if I'm going to be a person of the world I'm going to embrace the full range of possible sexual experiences. He stupidly convinces himself he must do it. That could work.

CALEB: You think so?

DAVID: But the ending—that's a startling gesture that I just don't buy.

CALEB: You don't buy it?

DAVID: Because I wouldn't do that.

CALEB: You wouldn't?

DAVID: No—I'm very self-protective. But I want to be convinced that another human being could do it even if I wouldn't. Is the narrator secretly bisexual? Is he self-annihilating? Or is he under the strong influence of a PC pan-globalism? He thinks, "I must experience everything." To me, that's you.

○

CALEB: What really happened is quite different. Eliza combines elements of a few girls I've known, including Marcy Lezcano.

DAVID: Marcy Lezcano?!

CALEB: Yes.

DAVID: She's part of all this?

CALEB: Indirectly. I took two novel classes with you, and Marcy was in both. I found her attractive, didn't you?

DAVID: Sure—that dark hair, her cigarettes, her husky voice, her fallen-angelness.

CALEB: I asked her out after the last day of the fall quarter. She gave me her number. When I called, her roommate told me Marcy was in the shower, took my name and number. Marcy didn't call back.

DAVID: Ouch.

CALEB: I take another class with you spring quarter; first day I come a few minutes early, and there's Marcy.

DAVID: Hello . . .

CALEB: We exchanged awkwardities, and as class goes on we're pleasant. The phone call is never mentioned. Then, later, she invites me to this party.

DAVID: She invited me, too. I didn't go.

CALEB: You? She's inviting her teacher? Cool, but jeez. The party was at a bar downtown.

DAVID: Yep.

CALEB: I went. It was a big setup, and I thought I might chat with Marcy, but I ended up meeting this girl. Marcy exits the story at this point.

DAVID: What did this other girl look like?

CALEB: The one in the story, the Samoan, was gorgeous; this one, not so much. We dance, even make out on the floor. She asked if I wanted to go to her place, we took a cab to this apartment on Capitol Hill, and then I found out it was a guy.

DAVID: How did you find out?

CALEB: By grabbing his hard penis.

DAVID: Yikes.

CALEB: I said, "I thought you were a girl. I was looking forward to having heterosexual sex." And I let him touch me, and I kept touching him, even kissing, but we just stopped. I said, "I'm too drunk." I didn't want to hurt his feelings—it sounds corny, but that's how I felt. I rolled over and passed out.

DAVID: I understand: you didn't want to be an asshole about it.

CALEB: I even had breakfast with him the next day.

DAVID: You slept in the same bed?

CALEB: On the floor. He spread blankets on the floor.

DAVID: But you didn't have sex?

CALEB: He starts to go down on me, but my cock's flaccid. It's, well, it's not Oedipus, but it's like I just found out the girl I'm fucking is my mother.

DAVID: Were his feelings hurt?

CALEB: I think he thought I was really too drunk. He's asking me if this is my first "experience" and I'm telling him I thought he was really a girl. He asks, "Then why are you here?" He wants to talk about it, get to know me.

DAVID: So that was the genesis of your story. There wasn't any Polynesian, or was there?

CALEB: Three years later, winter of 1994, I fly to Apia in Western Samoa (Maugham set "Rain" in Pago Pago, American Samoa). I get off the plane, and my story describes it exactly, right down to the sign in the airport: "Keep Our Country AIDS Free."

I get a room, drop off my bags, walk around town, and this very beautiful woman hits on me. We make a date for late afternoon, and I go back to the hostel to get ready. At the hostel there's a group of travelers, a Maori couple, an Australian gal, a German guy, a Norwegian, and his temporary Samoan girlfriend, Noella. Noella is key.

DAVID: Is she a transvestite, too?

CALEB: No. Six people—too many names to keep track of, but whenever I remember this story, I think of them. The Maori guy was called Lucky. Carol the Australian, Bernhard the German, and Vagard the Norwegian with Noella. We're all talking and sharing stories, and they're going out that night and ask me to come. I say, great, but I'm meeting this girl. So we all end up going out: these six people, me, and my date.

DAVID: Does everyone know she's a transvestite?

CALEB: The point is I don't. She's really hot. I can't take my eyes off her. I mean supermodel hot. I'm thinking I've got the hottest woman in this dance club.

DAVID: And she's Polynesian?

CALEB: Samoan. I don't even suspect, even though I've been fooled before.

DAVID: By Marcy Lezcano.

CALEB: By her friend.

DAVID: Right.

CALEB: She's telling me I'm gorgeous. At this time I had long hair; she loves my long hair.

DAVID: Right.

CALEB: I'm just a mimbo.

DAVID: What's a mimbo—a man bimbo?

CALEB: A Seinfeldism. We're dancing on the floor, and whenever my date goes to the bathroom, all my new friends compliment me. The Maori couple, especially. Lucky and his girlfriend kept saying, "You're such a beautiful couple. You really go well together." They bought us a couple rounds of drinks. And all of us are dancing.

DAVID: Four couples.

CALEB: Yep. Then everyone leaves, and it's just me and this transvestite. We go off in a corner of the dance club and have a drink. It's dark and secluded, and she goes under the table and starts giving me a blow job. I come. And we set up a date for the next day.

DAVID: When she gave you a blow job, wasn't there any "Turnabout is fair play; now I'll please you"?

CALEB: I tried. Not going down but to touch. She pulled my hand away, wouldn't let me touch her, not even her breasts. She didn't let me put my hands underneath her clothes, and I did think, This is really weird.

DAVID: She said she just liked to give pleasure.

CALEB: She said it was fun. I paid for everything—drinks, dinner, her cab home. I even suggested coming back to the room, but she wanted to go home, meet the next day. At the time, I didn't know the hostel had a policy and wouldn't have let her in, and that's why she didn't want to come. The next day I'm hanging out with the gang at the hostel, and they ask me about my girlfriend, and I say, "We're going out tonight, too." And then Noella asks me if I know it's a guy.

DAVID: Out of nowhere.

CALEB: Out of nowhere. I'm like, "Blaaaaaaaaaahggg!" I ask Noella, "Are you joking?"

DAVID: How could she tell it was a guy?

CALEB: Duh. She was Samoan. It turns out they all knew.

DAVID: How old were you?

CALEB: Twenty-five.

DAVID: Pretty young.

CALEB: Old enough to know better. I ask Noella, "Why

didn't you tell me earlier?" She shrugs. I'd planned to meet this transvestite by the hostel, she's due any second, and I say, "Well, she's coming here, so let's get out of here before she arrives." We leave, and the transvestite is outside. She's waving and hollers, "Yoo-hoo! Caleb!"

I start shaking my head, and I say, "Forget it. No. Go home. No."

She just starts laughing. "Oh, you found out I'm a fag!" The only thing I'm thinking is how glad I am I'm overseas and no one will ever know this story.

DAVID: And everyone knew?

CALEB: Everyone. Later, Bernhard, the German, hits on me: "In my home country I drive BMW. Sex with guy, sex with girl, vat's the difference? If you vant to have sex with me, why not? I zee no problem." Vagard, Bernhard, Noella, and I go eat at this Chinese dive; Vagard tells me the same thing happened to him.

DAVID: What?

CALEB: Before he met Noella, the same transvestite had tried to pick up Vagard. He said, "She wanted to go to a bar, and we get a couple drinks and head toward the back, where she starts giving me a blow job. I try to touch her, but she won't let me. I'm thinking, What woman doesn't want to be touched? I say, 'You're a guy, aren't you?' "

Vagard had traveled through Southeast Asia, and transvestites were all over the place: they tuck themselves, get implants, fake boobs, and they still have Adam's apples and big hands. He put two and two together. When I tried to add two and two, I came up with around nineteen.

David laughs.

CALEB: Not only Vagard and Noella but everyone knew, and the transvestite knew everyone knew, and everyone knew that the transvestite knew they knew. There was probably a lot of weird energy going on, and I was just oblivious. The transvestite probably was wondering, How does this Caleb guy still not know?

DAVID: And she's not doing it for money?

CALEB: At the end, she asked for cab fare. I said how much? And she said ten dollars. Seemed reasonable.

Finally, everyone flies off to wherever, and now it's just me and Noella. It's afternoon and we go out, have a bite, and I tell Noella everything, including the fact that I got a blow job. She tells me about how they trick foreigners all the time. Some get paid; sometimes the foreigners know and don't care. Even locals get blow jobs.

Noella and I hang out all day, and in one afternoon she tells me her entire life story, as much life story as you can tell in one afternoon. She went to college in Australia on a scholarship, had a boyfriend, fell in love, got pregnant, but the boyfriend didn't want to marry. Her visa expired, so she came back to Samoa and gave birth.

I tell her I'm thinking of switching to a different hostel and I ask if she wants to come with me. She asks me, "So you want to have fun tonight?" Now, she's been sleeping with this Norwegian guy all week, and she knows I had been with the Samoan transvestite.

DAVID: Wasn't she worried about getting AIDS?

CALEB: Evidently not. She has this sad life.

DAVID: Did she have any ulterior motive for wanting to have this brief affair with you?

CALEB: Of course she might have been fishing for more. Who knows? She claimed that local guys weren't interested in her because of her situation. She was matter-of-fact: *nothing I can do.* She radiated benevolence, or so it seemed at the time, especially in my memory.

There I am, just happy she doesn't see me as a long-haired idiot who's been dancing with a transvestite. I'm thinking she's got low standards: "I wouldn't want to be in a club that would have me as a member."

Making love to her was an incredibly beautiful experience—a release, a way to move on, but I was moving on. I was definitely the more selfish between the two of us. She went with me to the airport, and rather than change my *talas* I gave them to her. The equivalent of seventy dollars. I never got an AIDS test until I worked in the United Arab Emirates.

DAVID: Let me get all these dates right.

CALEB: In 1991 I had the experience with the transvestite at the birthday party. Noella had her son and left Australia in 1991. In 1994 I had the second transvestite experience and met Noella. I got the AIDS test in 1997.

DAVID: Hmm. To be blunt, there are two things about you as a person that especially interest me.

CALEB: Only two?

DAVID: Part of you is very knowledgeable and insightful, and part of you is stunningly blind to your own affect.

CALEB: Maybe that's who I am. If so, I'm doomed. I can't change.

DAVID: I'm sure you could say the same thing about me.

CALEB: Of course, I think I am aware of my obliviousness, but it's a contradiction. If I am oblivious, then how could I be aware of it? When an author starts questioning, it drags the story down. It's aesthetic. You may say the opposite.

DAVID: Completely, because to me there's no separation between—

CALEB: You want questioning of the self, and memory, and so on. All memoirists do it.

DAVID: I'm not a memoirist. None of the writers I love are memoirists. I'm interested in the book-length essay.

CALEB: Distinction without a difference.

DAVID: You don't know what you're talking about.

CALEB: I'm trying to get at suffering, why people suffer, and how they can stop suffering. Maybe I haven't perfected my craft, but that's my goal—not an endlessly self-reflexive questioning of self.

DAVID: And that's why your work still feels to me pretty generic: because you haven't learned how to wire the investigation through the central intelligence agency of your own sensibility. Without that, it's just something coming in over telex.

CALEB: Telex?

DAVID: I was flashing on *Swimming to Cambodia,* for some reason. I've been totally riveted by the story—who wouldn't be? But it never, in my hearing, really built to anything, about you or sex or suffering. You gotta get to your own obtuseness. The way—let me finish, Caleb—the way I'd write it is this: Here's a guy who has a peculiar experience at a birthday party, then he has another experience in

Samoa with a transvestite who gives him a blow job. Everyone teases him—ha ha. Then, to me, the really interesting
moment is his brief connection with Noella. That should
have been the aha moment for you, but it wasn't. Maybe
this is my own Western prejudice or heterosexual prejudice, but wasn't she hoping that you would take care of her
in some sense?

CALEB: Damn straight. There's a magazine in Bangkok called
Farang. Phnom Penh, Taiwan, Korea—half the travel literature in Asia is about this. Somaly Mam, the author of *The
Road of Lost Innocence*, married a john, a Frenchman working for an NGO in Phnom Penh. She wanted to be saved,
and he wanted to save someone, but they started off as Mr.
John and Mrs. Whore, no sugarcoating. All over Asia, and
the world, there are women like Somaly or Noella, all at
various stages of wanting to be saved.

DAVID: Were you attracted to Noella?

CALEB: I rate women on a binary scale: either zero or one.
She was a one.

DAVID: *(laughing)* I'm sure you have equally devastating
insights into me, but you're a funny mix of gentleness and
obstreperousness. You sometimes seem belligerent, but
you're also compassionate. You're very interested in culture. You're a better anthropologist of the world than most
of us are. But the story, or the essay, has to build to either
(1) you remain studiously oblivious in three cases, and the
reader gets that, or (2) you yourself finally confront in yourself your own blindness.

CALEB: Hmm.

DAVID: I think you're very smart, but underneath that you're stupid, whereas I'm very stupid, but underneath that I'm smart.

CALEB: I almost think our conversation about the story might be, in essence, the story.

DAVID: Ooh, I like that.

CALEB: What did you mean, though, when you said you think I'm a funny mix—

DAVID: Calling me a "dork," say—why would you do that?

CALEB: *(laughing)* I was toning it down.

○

DAVID: What happened to your face?

CALEB: The scars? Car accident. July 1985: I was sixteen. I'd been invited to a Chicago Cubs tryout camp at Skagit Valley Community College. All the local prospects were there—mostly college. It was before my senior year of high school. I'd been an all-league pitcher. Everyone did sprints and played catch and then played a simulated game. I pitched two innings, didn't allow a hit—not much of a sample, but it got a scout, Andy Pienovi, interested. He talked to me and gave me his card.

DAVID: So you could throw a ninety-mile-per-hour fastball?

CALEB: Mid-eighties. I weighed about 160 pounds but had an odd delivery and could put English on the ball. I worked nights at a restaurant and always smoked pot afterward and sometimes got drunk. Couple weeks later I was driving home from work, probably high and drunk, and I ran into a tree. Scars on my face, broke my arm, some vertebrae, and my brain. I was flown by helicopter to St. Luke's in Bellingham, in a coma for four days, and in the hospital for two months. This factored in my early writing. Mark and Vince lost their parents. They saw death, but I almost died.

○

CALEB: What's so great about Jackson Pollock?

DAVID: His work is unspeakably beautiful, and he changed the history of art. Other than that, not much.

CALEB: I'd argue he changed art negatively. Why do you find his work beautiful?

DAVID: More than anyone before him, he showed you the artist in the process of making art. He showed you—

CALEB: Whoop-de-fucking-do.

DAVID: I share your skepticism. I hate art talk. But I honestly respond to Pollock, Diebenkorn, Rothko. I just do. Most artists do nothing for me—de Kooning, say. Visual art is completely visceral: I love Gerhard Richter's work—immediately upon looking at it. You either get, I don't know, Rauschenberg, or you don't. I love collage, so I do.

CALEB: "You either get it or you don't" is a brick wall. You either get Christianity or you don't. You either get French wines or you don't. Or Franzen. Basically, you're saying, "If you can't see value, it's your fault." We both agree the Cascade Mountains are beautiful, but Pollock?

DAVID: To me, the Cascade Mountains are nowhere near as beautiful as a painting by Jackson Pollock.

CALEB: Now you're just being stupid.

○

CALEB: In one corner we have Eula Biss's *The Balloonists*, seventy-two pages of lyric essay. In the opposite corner we have Eula Biss's *Notes from No Man's Land*, winner of the National Book Critics Circle Award. David Shields speaks for the former. Caleb Powell speaks for the latter.

DAVID: I like both books.

CALEB: You said you were surprised *No Man's Land* won that award.

DAVID: I like the book. I don't love it anything like the way I love *The Balloonists*. You know this line of Picasso's I always quote? "A great painting comes together, just barely." That, for me, is the definition of art. The casual reader reads *The Balloonists* and has no idea what it's about, whereas *No Man's Land* pretty much spells it out; there's nothing to get. *The Balloonists* is this incredible generation-defining anthem about how Eula simply can't get the hot-air balloon of romance off the ground, because she just can't believe in it anymore, not after everything she's seen happen to her mother.

CALEB: *(laughing)* Big fucking deal.

DAVID: Is that right? To you, that's—

CALEB: We're endlessly dreaming about being in a balloon?

This balloon will save us? That's an X factor? I'm chewing gum as I'm tasting wine.

○

CALEB: The artist has to have a foot in the world, be open to journalism, expository writing. I'm a writer first, artist second. You may be the opposite. I want writing to mix artistic with nonartistic, to link to interest in human crises. Hitchens or Samantha Power or Jon Krakauer on Mormon fundamentalists who commit a brutal murder. Orwell's good, because he combined a great writing style with firsthand knowledge of the world. The microphone didn't catch that, but when I mentioned Krakauer, David Shields gave a "yuck" face and a thumbs-down gesture.

DAVID: Two thumbs down.

CALEB: He's a writer first and an artist second.

DAVID: When I talk about Chomsky, I paint in very broad strokes and I sound foolish, since I don't care sufficiently about the details. I don't care as much about politics as you do. When you talk about Pollock, you paint in very broad strokes and you sound foolish, since you don't care sufficiently about the details. You don't care as much as I do about art.

CALEB: You don't sound that foolish regarding Chomsky; you're too aware of your own ignorance. I hoped you might go to the mat for Chomsky; things would have gotten heated. If I sound foolish to some people, so be it, but I have a sophisticated distaste for Pollock. My mother was a painter. I grew up around painting and art history books. I've engaged. I care about the details. His work is crap.

○

CALEB: Maggie Nelson, Sarah Manguso, Amy Fusselman, Simon Gray, Leonard Michaels, David Markson: I like all these writers you like. In Fusselman's *The Pharmacist's Mate*, when she finally gets pregnant, she ties this in with memories of her father and her desire to have a baby. It was a satisfying book.

DAVID: You're flattening the book down to nothing. It's not about her getting pregnant. The book is held together by this extraordinary trope: all three tracks—her father as a pharmacist's mate, her attempt to get pregnant, and her father dying—are about the gossamer-thin difference between life and death. That's what holds the book together.

CALEB: Okay . . .

DAVID: It's crucial to me that these books rotate outward toward a metaphor. In *Bluets*, Nelson is obsessed with the color blue, can't get over her ex-boyfriend, and her friend is paralyzed. She's asking a series of related questions: Why are we so sad? Why is the human animal so melancholy? How do we deal with loss? How do we deal with the ultimate loss?—which is death. It's actively about the intersection of these things.

CALEB: I find *Bluets* much more interesting when she's talking about her paralyzed friend, when she's showing empathy. The poetic meanderings on blue and the Tuareg and cyan and sadness, not so much. And this painful breakup: he's two-timing her. That, to me, is obliviousness of obliviousness. What's her point? She's having mega-erotic passionate sex. Enjoy it, baby. Don't bring me your pain. Give me widows of Kabul, give me Krakauer's psychopaths, give me a Khmer Rouge cadre cutting off Haing Ngor's finger, give me Texas death row inmates, give me Somaly Mam getting fucked in a brothel by a former soldier who lost an arm and an eye, give me Maggie's quadriplegic friend, give me painful pain.

○

DAVID: In your story, what's the takeaway? What are you saying about sexuality in the West and East and desire and oppression and obliviousness and risk? The point is what? What do you think that story is saying? What are you saying?

CALEB: Right now I'm not saying anything.

DAVID: If you just need time to think . . .

CALEB: You're much more certain about literature than I am. You say Fusselman's book is about the gossamer-thin difference between life and death. Fine, but everything is about that. When you're alive and can die at any moment, and the people you love can die at any moment, and people who starve or are bombed can die at any moment, or death row prisoners can die at any moment, and every day people do die, that's the gossamer-thin difference between life and death. I rarely get this tension from the books you write or the books you love.

○

CALEB: You express your aesthetic well—that's your strength. You talk about these other books and turn back to yourself, and thus you aspire to do what you admire.

DAVID: No, that's backward! I write what I write and then I find work that deepens and extends my aesthetic.

CALEB: Can you talk without me? I've got to go to the bathroom.

DAVID: *(to the DVR)* Okay, back at the ranch: I want to say to Caleb, "I'm not only good at cutting to the essence of a work of literature. I hope that's a strength of mine in general, as a person." I think it is. Laurie gave me a birthday card last year that said, "Thanks for being so good at analyzing things and resolving disputes." Uh, what's my point? Essences are what I'm interested in, which is the whole reason I'm interested in literary collage: I love exquisitely compressed riffs, shards—

CALEB: *(returning)* Khamta said we should try Lake Elizabeth.

DAVID: A hike?

CALEB: We can get there by road and then we can walk around the lake.

DAVID: Great. Lunch in town, then the lake. And we can go back to Cascadia tonight.

◐

CALEB: *(skimming a newspaper at the Skykomish Public Library)* They got Anwar al-Awlaki.

DAVID: It's funny: Obama is far more militarily effective than Bush.

CALEB: And Libya seems to have turned out okay.

DAVID: I guess.

CALEB: I'll turn this off.

◐

CALEB: My dad and I had problems getting along twenty years ago. I don't think we liked each other. He's prehistoric when it comes to race and homosexuality and so forth. This thinking dies out a little more with every generation; with him there's no point in debating. Now, he comes over, adores my daughters. I can watch them and feel at peace.

DAVID: What does he do with them?

CALEB: Takes them swimming or to the playground. I painted his house this summer, and he spent a lot of time with them. My mom's relatively useless, almost an extra burden. He has to take care of her, so he'll watch the kids and my mother will just sit at home with a magazine.

DAVID: As you get older, it matters more. It'd be hard to function without family. I know I couldn't.

CALEB: If you don't have a child, it's different: family has a different meaning. One of the most revealing things about you that I didn't know (and as far as I know, you haven't written about it) is that Laurie wanted to have a second child and you said no. A second child would have given Laurie a lot of joy.

DAVID: Me, too, for that matter.

CALEB: As well as Natalie. The idea of a fourteen- or fifteen-year-old kid at home. And the empty nest, rather than now, would happen when this youngest child goes to college in a couple years.

DAVID: Got it. . . . Do you wish you had had more kids?

CALEB: We're happy with three.

DAVID: Three's a lot.

CALEB: I got snipped.

DAVID: You're done.

CALEB: For two days afterward, every time my wife asked me to do anything I'd shout, "My balls, sorry, my balls! Now please bring me a bowl of ice cream."

DAVID: That'd be fun.

CALEB: It was. You've talked about Laurie asking for a second child, but what else don't I know about you? Are there any secrets that you've kept out of your writing?

DAVID: I'd talk about them if there were, but there's nothing I can think of right now, and I definitely want to get a good hike in before it gets dark.

○

CALEB: Have you ever betrayed someone?

DAVID: I've never had an affair outside of my marriage, if that's what you're asking. Have you?

CALEB: No.

DAVID: At these various conferences and residencies, you know, out of who knows what mixed motive, these girls come on to you.

CALEB: It's probably very tempting, especially for the single writer.

DAVID: If I do that, the marriage is effectively over. I'm not French.

CALEB: Get divorced first.

DAVID: But it's a nice test. I really do want a successful marriage.

CALEB: It's—I've been single. That was fun, but why be with someone you're willing to cheat on? Serial monogamy and then marriage.

DAVID: I've been thinking about these eighteen-year periods of my life. From zero to eighteen I was growing up, and eighteen to thirty-six I was more or less on my own, and thirty-six to fifty-four I was a husband and father. And now Natalie's eighteen and out of the house, so I'm starting to enter the fourth phase of my life. Natalie's part of our life, but she's one step removed, and it's been interesting.

Laurie and I had this discussion a couple of years ago. We weren't getting along that great, and I'm pretty sure she was under the influence of one of her friends who was getting divorced. We got into an argument about some minor thing—Oliver Stone's movie about Bush, actually—and found ourselves asking what we were going to do if and when Natalie left the house for school. We were saying our marriage is okay, but are we really happily married? "Let's give ourselves eighteen months. I don't think either of us is going to do anything until Natalie leaves for school, and if we're unhappily married then, we can act." It was a fascinating trial period. And I tried very, very hard to engage with Laurie, whether helping out in the kitchen, taking walks, trips, watching movies together, etc. It's—

CALEB: Sorry to interject, but I can see my marriage in this. It's an unavoidable dynamic.

DAVID: How so?

CALEB: Being involved in my own stuff, I don't need an outside source to share it with, especially if there's only superficial interest, and thus I can't share a lot with Terry. I wish she'd have her own passion so she could occupy herself. And maybe your marriage might be better if Laurie had more of that.

DAVID: I know I have major, major deficits as a spouse. I'm so wrapped up in my own head. Sometimes I suppose I wished she had an equally focused interest, but on the other hand she's great to me, in many ways. She has incredible "emotional intelligence," she helps me figure stuff out, she makes our house really nice. She's what used to be called—I hate this term—a "writer's wife." Maybe she was wearying of that. There's a way in which I was an old fifty-three and she was a young fifty-three. She's limber. She does yoga, Pilates—

CALEB: She certainly looks younger than she is.

DAVID: She's starting to let her hair grow in gray, and she's wearing glasses more; to me, she looks like an austere French intellectual (which I find incredibly sexy—her slight remove). She's in really great shape, but with my back woes I can't go on elaborate hiking trips, etc. We could have gone in a few directions. We could have, you know, just gone our separate ways. "We had a pretty good marriage, we raised Natalie, but we're too different." I'm not sure how much of this I articulated to her. Some of it was in my own mind. Then, there's another marriage where we keep on going as is and it's okay, but we agree to look the other way. The third option, the most interesting, is the one we're trying to do now: Okay, now let's try to be married for real. We were married for less than three years before Natalie was born.

CALEB: I still can't believe that you were together four years and never discussed kids. Another overworked chess metaphor, but before you move the "marriage chess piece," resolve the kid question.

DAVID: And I'd say again, "Life isn't a chess game, my friend."

○

CALEB: My parents celebrated their fifty-fourth anniversary earlier this year. Every year my mom says, "Dave and I have enjoyed—however many—years of blisssss . . . ters."

DAVID: Oof. I hate puns like that.

CALEB: And every time, my dad gets red in the face. My mom says, "Bliss . . ." She pauses and lets my dad react. He says, "Trice. Don't say it!" Then she drops the ". . . ssssters." I'll do this with my wife now and then, just to freak her out.

DAVID: Sometimes it does baffle me that Laurie and I married each other. She's very, very smart, but she's not intellectual—probably somewhat like Terry.

CALEB: I always say that she's smarter, and I'm stronger.

DAVID: Yep—me, too. With my bad back I can lift grand pianos.

CALEB: She earns the money. I move heavy objects. She loves family time. All weekend it's "Let's do this, let's do that." And we spend the whole weekend doing this and that: going to the zoo, parks, movies. She just loves "being a family."

DAVID: You wish she'd take the kids more often.

CALEB: No. Yes. No. Well, yes. She works all week, she deserves to call the shots on the weekend, but I wouldn't mind having more time to myself.

DAVID: She doesn't put a huge priority on your writing.

CALEB: My writing doesn't bring anything into the family. I'm not as good a father and a husband if I'm doing something that doesn't bring in income, so I carve out writing moments early in the morning or late at night, and now two of the kids are in elementary school, so I have more time.

DAVID: I'm still not someone who makes huge amounts of money, but I get these lecture gigs now: I go somewhere for a day or two or three and get paid two, three, five thousand dollars.

CALEB: People pay money to listen to you gab?

DAVID: I go to a college, critique manuscripts, give a lecture, a reading, do a Q&A, visit classes.

CALEB: Hey, this is cool: on the map they have paved roads, groomed dirt roads, and trails.

DAVID: Why do we need a map—to make sure we don't fall? . . . Anyway, the point is it took forever, and I finally make enough money writing and teaching and talking about writing that—

CALEB: You can move to a better house.

DAVID: What's the matter with my house?

CALEB: I was joking!

DAVID: So was I!

CALEB: You can travel more, indulge.

DAVID: A little. I have three more years of Natalie's tuition and that's $57K a year. I also want to make enough money that Laurie can maybe open a café. She's a great cook.

CALEB: That'd be so—

DAVID: She'd love it.

CALEB: Many restaurants aren't literally losing money. The owners just can't survive on what they make. Sometimes they make less than the dishwasher. They have a $2,000 mortgage, a couple kids, car payments, business loans, and they can't get by on what amounts to a $20,000 salary.

DAVID: It's hard to make a profit, definitely. Before, I wasn't very supportive of her idea to quit Fred Hutch, and now I'm just, "Go for it." I really want my marriage to work, and if it collapsed I'd be devastated, so I've made a really concerted gesture to meet her halfway.

CALEB: You da man.

DAVID: I don't know about your marriage—whether you've ever hit a wall and said, "Here we are; do we want to be married?"

CALEB: We've hit different walls. Three kids is a lot.

DAVID: You're almost too busy.

CALEB: The physical life suffers.

DAVID: So I've heard.

CALEB: It shouldn't be a surprise that when you have kids you lose that spontaneity.

DAVID: Do you guys ever go off, alone, to a hotel for a weekend?

CALEB: Every now and then we get a date weekend.

○

CALEB: Funny coincidence: when I painted Gayle Anne's house, she said you're one of her store's best customers.

DAVID: I'll send her an email, and the next day her husband will drop the book off on my front porch. She out-Amazons Amazon.

CALEB: She and her husband went to Bermuda for ten days and gave me keys to their house. What's that Raymond Carver story where the guy house-sits, ends up wearing his neighbor's lingerie, moves stuff around, and then locks himself out? I'm not that guy, but it's tough not to look.

DAVID: You get a sense of their life?

CALEB: Wall-to-wall books. He's got a room full of guitars, not many family photos, but they have a picture of a baby, and by the coloration it's at least thirty years old. That's it. One picture.

DAVID: I always get the feeling they don't have kids, but perhaps they did.

CALEB: The question: did the baby die?

DAVID: "For Sale: Baby Shoes, never worn."

CALEB: Some people want to talk about tragedy, some don't, and I'm certainly not close enough to Gayle Ann to ask her. Maybe I'm just way off. . . . Hold on. Maybe we should turn around.

DAVID: They should have a sign saying "Four-Wheel Drive Only."

CALEB: My wheels might not survive.

DAVID: I wonder how close we are. I might be kidding myself. Is the danger a punctured tire?

CALEB: That's a danger. I almost hope it happens. You'll change it.

DAVID: Ha ha. Let's see. This is much farther than I realized. I wonder when it'll get dark—seven or so? It's now four.

CALEB: I'm going to be a wimp and pull over. We can continue on foot.

○

CALEB: This summer my mother asked me what I wanted for my birthday. I wanted a portrait of my daughters. She ended up painting three black-and-white doodles. I said, "This? It took you fifteen minutes." My father said, "No,

Caleb, it took your mother her entire life." He's right. The caricatures are adorable, the kids like them, and they're the best my mother could do.

DAVID: Is she senile?

CALEB: Happy-senile. Whether she dies in a year or ten, it's over. She's a borderline diabetic: cholesterol and glucose off the charts; her doctors have warned her about sugar, but she's an addict. A while ago we had popsicles in the fridge, and she wanted one. The agreed-upon rule for her is one treat a day. She'd already had a cinnamon roll for breakfast. We gave the girls popsicles, and a couple minutes later Ava comes running into the kitchen, crying. "Grandma took my popsicle." We go into the living room and it's true. My mom's slurping on Ava's popsicle.

DAVID: What can you do but throw up your hands and laugh?

CALEB: Mentally, my father is fine, but he has aneurysms and pre-leukemia, a pacemaker. He's had fainting spells.

DAVID: This is incredibly embarrassing, but I want to live longer than my father, who died four months short of his ninety-ninth birthday.

○

DAVID: Pessoa, *The Book of Disquiet*: "I weep over nothing that life brings or takes away, but there are pages of prose that have made me cry."

CALEB: You can live in both. Both can make you cry.

DAVID: No you can't.

CALEB: Maybe *you* can't.

DAVID: I live more totally through writing than you do. I make more sacrifices.

CALEB: I'd say my sacrifices aren't less, just different.

DAVID: You are—this is an old-fashioned word, and I don't know if I'm willing to say it—but you're more "soulful." I'll do anything to protect my writing, and I'll do anything to get a book done. I'm ruthless about it, while you, I think, err on the side of experience, of pleasure. Life.

CALEB: I haven't had enough time to think about it, but let me use the word "monstrous" to describe you not yielding to Laurie's desire to have a second child.

DAVID: That really seems brutal to you? That's interesting.

CALEB: You used the word "difficult" to describe Natalie's first two years of existence. To me, those years were an incredibly happy period. Every time my baby cried, even at three a.m., she was saying, "I love you I need you I love you." When Ava was two months old, I'd put her in my front pack and walk around the neighborhood with this warm, semiconscious living creature bundled against my chest. That's meaning. That's an X factor. Those are good memories.

DAVID: Not sure what to say other than "We're different."

CALEB: For me to accuse you of being a monster—that's unfair, perhaps. You had doubts and made a responsible decision. Who am I to say? And how does Laurie feel?

DAVID: As I say, she acknowledges that she was ambivalent at the time. . . . The lake?

CALEB: Runoff stream.

DAVID: We'll walk until—what was my point?

CALEB: About how Laurie was ambivalent, but she's—

DAVID: When we dropped off Natalie at college, Laurie said she wished we had a child to come home to. I did, too. Laurie's amazing, though. She gets great satisfaction from being of service to other people and—I don't know what to say—I get great satisfaction from being served.

David and Caleb laugh.

○

CALEB: The girls like to get their fingernails painted.

DAVID: Natalie used to love Build-A-Bear.

CALEB: They love Build-A-Bear. If I had a son, I'd spend more time on sports and less on writing. I'm not saying this would be bad. I'm looking at the positive side of having girls, but my girls are horrible at sports and they have no interest. Last year we signed them up for T-ball. Ava's six and Gia's five. They just want to play with their friends; they couldn't care less about learning to catch and throw. Some parents stay engaged. They rah-rah the whole time.

DAVID: That can get wearisome.

CALEB: There's a kid on third base, her teammate hits the ball to left field, and she runs after the ball in left field instead of running home. Stuff like that.

DAVID: That's adorable; I could watch that all day.

○

CALEB: You have a sister, but you don't talk about her much. Or write about her. All you do is mention the fact you have one.

DAVID: Let me tie my shoes. My sister, Paula, is a year older. Someone once asked me, "Are you an only child?" And I remember thinking, Whoa! Do I seem like an only child? Paula and I don't get along at all, but she's close to Natalie.

CALEB: Does she have kids?

DAVID: No. She and her husband, Wayne, live in Tacoma. He teaches history at PLU [Pacific Lutheran University], and she studied for a doctorate in history at Berkeley but never finished her dissertation.

CALEB: Just like my mother, who stopped six months short of her Ph.D. in Chinese studies at Columbia. It's odd anyone would get that close and give up.

DAVID: Paula has worked for more than twenty-five years in the UW admissions office.

CALEB: Why don't the two of you get along?

DAVID: First, I think, she's an older sister; no matter what happens, she always treats me like her younger brother, and I probably act like her younger brother. She also really resents that I've written about our family.

CALEB: Aha.

DAVID: That's a big thing. Even writing about her obliquely is—

CALEB: She plays such a minor role.

DAVID: I honestly would love to ask Paula—maybe I

will—what I've done to make her so rancorous toward me, but when she and I are in the same room together, the air positively vibrates with hostility. When we were kids, she was quite the academic star. And I was, if not the dumb jock, the barely sentient jock. Whenever I did good work, my teachers would accuse me of having had her do it for me. Or they'd say, "It's so hard to believe you're Paula's brother." She's never found a calling equal to her intelligence, while I, for better and worse, have known what I wanted to do since I was twelve. This is all wildly self-serving on my part, but I think she takes her disappointment over her lack of a "career" and channels it into resentment of me. I also think she and I tend to replicate exactly the completely fucked-up dynamic between my mother and my—

CALEB: Oh!

DAVID: You okay? Did you twist your knee?

CALEB: Hit a slippery spot on that log. I'm okay.

DAVID: Paula and Wayne will be over at our house, and whenever I say something she disagrees with, which is pretty much all the time, she'll look over at him and roll her eyes.

One time, after *Black Planet* was published, she meant to send an email to Wayne and accidentally sent it to me: "See, I knew he was thinking that, I told you so, ha ha, he's such a hypocrite." I wrote back, "Uh, hi, Paula. I think you sent your email to the wrong person."

Caleb laughs.

DAVID: Then I said, "I don't think we have a very good relationship. We just don't get along. Why don't we get together and talk about why that's so? Let's try to be honest with each other." And she said, "I can't do that." I may well be mistaken, but I took that to mean, "I'm not together enough to do that." Christ, I'd love to hear her version of all this, which I'm sure is equally devastating. Tell me about your siblings.

○

CALEB: My youngest sister, Min, and her husband, Somjait, are 9/11 Truthers, question the moon landing, don't vaccinate their kids, homeschool, think 150 rich families control the world.

DAVID: A hundred and fifty rich families probably do control the world.

CALEB: I'll have them send you pamphlets. Every year it's something different. They stock up on water purification tablets and pandemic ventilators. It's intellecticide. This summer, when the Birthers were questioning whether Obama is American, I joked to Terry, "I'll bet you Min and Somjait buy into that." They do.

DAVID: Are they as conservative as your parents?

CALEB: They caucus for Ron Paul.

DAVID: He's not that awful.

CALEB: What? You like Wrong Paul?

DAVID: I didn't say that. I like his desire to reduce the military. As with Chomsky, I have a lot of problems with him, but I like backbench flamethrowers.

○

CALEB: Too much or too little frequency harms a relationship, especially in a marriage.

DAVID: Tell me about it.

CALEB: I call it being Wapatoed. We've stayed at vacation rentals in Wapato Point at Lake Chelan three times. Terry likes it because it's child-friendly, has outdoor and indoor pools, a hot tub, decent price, cheap boat rentals, miniature golf, and isn't so nice that we have to worry about the kids destroying the place. Terry uses it as a model for every vacation. Whenever I hear something for the zillionth time, I'll say, "Wapato." When I tell Terry about "David Shields Weekend," she'll say, "Wapato." You probably have the same thing with Laurie.

DAVID: Basically, I have seventy-six stories and I've told them all twenty-two times.

CALEB: "My student's prison stories were too stoical." "I read my ex-girlfriend's diary." "Writing is my revenge on stuttering." "Franzen is writing novels from 1850." "And I sure like Renata Adler's *Speed*—"

DAVID: Moo!

Caleb laughs.

DAVID: It's one of the things you're not supposed to like about marriage, but I do: it's hard to surprise each other after a while.

CALEB: Kundera says, "Happiness is a longing for repetition."

DAVID: I must be really, really happy, then, because my life is *Groundhog Day*, and I can't wait to get up every morning.

○

CALEB: It's always interesting to me when religious people cite the benefits of an afterlife as proof of an afterlife. I'll concede that eternal peaceful life is a pleasant thought. So? What consolation for me? When I die, I want the knowledge that I've lived well, that family and love and art will continue.

DAVID: You don't find that death haunts you on a daily level?

CALEB: I'm a secular moralist, so of course I think about it often.

DAVID: I want to believe the idea that by the time you're old enough to die it doesn't seem quite so awful. . . . What's that, a motorcycle?

CALEB: How you guys doing?

DIRT BIKER ONE: Good. How are you?

DAVID: Good.

DIRT BIKER TWO: You gonna check out the mine?

CALEB: Mine? How far?

DIRT BIKER ONE: Half-mile.

DIRT BIKER TWO: Not even. Two hundred yards. It's awesome freaky.

DAVID: Really?

DIRT BIKER ONE: Just go up there. Can't miss it. Got some flashlights?

DIRT BIKER TWO: It's big and deep and dark.

CALEB: We'll check it out.

DAVID: Have a good one.

DIRT BIKER TWO: You, too.

○

CALEB: Here we are, the entrance to the mine: corrugated sheet metal, rotted timbers. You would need a flashlight. All right, I'm going in. This is a legend I heard from the bartender at the Cascadia. It's supposedly true, or at least the Skykomish folk believe it. *(Caleb clicks on flip camera—footsteps on gravel)*

The Skykomish Witch Project: In 1921 a local miner, John Rockwell, discovered his wife and best friend in a compromising position outside the Whistling Post. Rockwell walked home, got his rifle and truck, returned, and drove them to this here mine. At gunpoint he led them inside and shot them dead. Or so he thought.

The next day he drank a fifth of whiskey, went downtown, and boasted that he killed his wife and that son-of-a-bitch friend. The police took John in for questioning. John took the police back to this very mine—to the site of the supposed murders. They found blood, but neither of the corpses. Three sets of footprints went in; only one set came out. Dogs followed the trail, but the deeper they went in, the more confused they became. They never found the bodies.

John went to trial and was convicted of this crime of passion. He served eight years, returned, became the town drunk, went crazy, and heard voices. John couldn't hold a job, even when the mines were busy. Two years later he hanged himself.

Little by little most Skykomish folk forgot about John

Rockwell, but in 1952 two hikers from California came to this mine, went inside with a flashlight, and came upon two people making love. Watching them was a man, hanging from the ceiling by his neck.

DAVID: Oooh. Shiver me timbers.

○

CALEB: I've been corresponding for over ten years with this Egyptian woman, Ceza, from when I lived in the UAE. Snail mail, email, Facebook. Ceza became a doctor, lived in the West, went to extremes with drugs, sex (with men and women), returned to Islam, but she always insisted on wearing the scarf. During the Arab Spring her friend was murdered, and the trial is fascinating. We discuss all this as a secular man and a Muslim woman.

DAVID: You wouldn't believe how many people think I'm going to be interested in their memoir. I'm not. I'm not interested in memoir. How does that V. S. Pritchett line go? "It's all in the art. You get no credit for living." A book doesn't become good because you were bad or had bad things done to you. If you can't transmute it into art, I'm not interested in it.

CALEB: One of the best "bad" books I've read is a memoir. The atrocious writing would be difficult to replicate. It was written by two women who did time with Mary Kay Letourneau. Self-published, but it sold well. An editor could have done wonders. I don't care much about Mary Kay, who's a one-page Wikipedia entry. These two women were far more compelling. One had been a stripper and murdered someone. The other was a drug addict who kept writing bad checks and embezzling. They took turns writing chapters. The stripper had been a willing fuck toy for her older brother's friends at the age of twelve. This made her feel dirty and helpless, destroyed her self-esteem. Neither woman could transmute their pain into art, but boy, do they make it real. And part of this reality was that they were really bad writers.

DAVID: I think that's an incredible story. Sex is always serious. It just is.

○

DAVID: I have a Twitter feed. And a Facebook page that says, "Hey, David did this."

CALEB: A fan page.

DAVID: What's the other way I could interact?

CALEB: You could have relationships on equal footing. Be friends. It's not literal.

DAVID: But what does that mean? What would be the advantage of me changing? I suppose it'd feel more friendly. . . . Peter [Mountford] asked me about you.

CALEB: What'd you say?

DAVID: I said Caleb will get in your face, and that's what

makes him a lively opponent. That's why I thought you and I would be a good fit for this, or are you like that only with me?

CALEB: No. Terry will vouch.

DAVID: Did you do that with Lidia? Or Ander? Or Eula?

CALEB: Not much. Their books didn't have much of an argument. Lidia's left-wing certain. Ander's talking about Frito-Lays and Americana and memoir and self. I think he shrinks from confrontation, which is usually fatal in a writer, but he makes it work. Eula's uncertain, concerned about the right things, and she's raising points that should be discussed. Do you know Patrick Madden?

DAVID: I've met him a couple of times.

CALEB: We're Facebook friends and he posted an article by Hitchens criticizing Mormons. I looked at the Hitchens article and then I wrote in the comment section on Madden's post: "Mormons have one too many *m*'s."

David laughs.

CALEB: Patrick writes, "That's not a very nice thing to say about a religion that fourteen million people believe in." I'm thinking, Hmm, not what I expected. So I write, "Nice, schmice." Then he writes, "So you insult me, my wife, my family, and my community?"

DAVID: Whoa.

CALEB: The back-and-forth isn't going the way I hoped. I go over the whole thread, dig up some info on Madden, and not only is he a Mormon but he converted. I can't tell him I didn't mean what I said, because I did, but I regret my attack and I want to convey this. I write an apology, saying that I respect him as a person and a writer and that my words and opinions had no place, given the spirit of the conversation. He writes an elegant reply—humble, understanding, kind, almost as if he's apologizing to me.

DAVID: There's something very substantial about him; you can feel that immediately. He's a mensch.

CALEB: I told him I'm universally disrespectful of religion— a vice that to me is a virtue—that I drink beer while my mother says grace, and when someone sneezes I say, "Imaginary Friend bless you."

DAVID: What'd he say?

CALEB: That he's had to deal with much worse.

○

CALEB: I get the feeling David Markson spends fifteen hours a day, seven days a week, reading and writing. I'm not sure how much experience he has with life.

DAVID: He died a year or two ago, but that's obviously a very scary model for myself.

CALEB: There's no way all those writers Markson romanticizes have mastered that many languages. It's like some actress can say *bonjour* and her publicity agent sells her as fluent in French.

DAVID: I find what you say reassuring, because I'm embarrassed that I've never gained true command of a second language. Even Nabokov's English is, to me, so phony. Markson calls it "the precious, pinchbeck, ultimately often flat prose of Vladimir Nabokov." All those twenty-dollar words of his, the enormous amount of alliteration. He actually has a really bad ear.

CALEB: I can forgive stilted language in Nabokov or Conrad or anyone who speaks a second language and writes intelligently. You've grown further and further away from Nabokov.

DAVID: Completely.

CALEB: You used to put him on a pedestal in class.

DAVID: I used to love his imperious distance. Now I hate it. There's never any blood on the page.

○

Returning on a forest service dirt road.

DAVID: I was staying in Mexico one summer, many years ago, writing *Dead Languages*. People at the hotel would ask me what I was doing and what the book was about, but I didn't have sufficiently good Spanish to explain this "literary" novel, so I made up this other book: *La casa del fuego*.

CALEB: Your Spanish was decent enough to communicate that?

DAVID: Each morning one of the waiters would ask me how my novel was coming along: "*¿Qué pasa con tu romance?*" And I'd say, "*¡Mi dios!*" Off I'd go on this fake novel. It was very basic—a melodramatic soap opera in which a house winds up burning down—but it was fun to "write."

I met this girl in Manzanillo at the beginning of the summer, when my Spanish was horrible. I visited her again in

Guadalajara at the end of the summer, and she couldn't believe we could actually communicate now. I'd spoken hardly any English in four and a half months.

CALEB: I'm surprised you don't spend more time in Mexico. *¿Balbuceas en español?*

DAVID: My Spanish was so faulty that if I stuttered, people thought I was simply having trouble with a foreign language, so it wasn't that evident. The moment I turned back to English, they'd notice that I spoke much faster in English.

CALEB: Speak English and you can teach and see the world.

DAVID: We're both lucky and unlucky we speak English.

CALEB: Shit!

DAVID: Uh-oh. That sounded bad. A puncture? Is that the main worry?

CALEB: I almost hope there's a flat. Jeez, David Shields can't change a flat.

DAVID: I don't keep picking up transvestites.

○

CALEB: The park service must have decided to throw a bunch of jagged stones in a ravine every hundred yards. Slowly but surely we made it. Hot tub?

DAVID: Sounds great. The Husky game is on, too.

CALEB: What time?

DAVID: They started at four. I wouldn't mind watching the last half, especially if they're in it. What time does the café close?

CALEB: The bar's open past midnight, but the kitchen closes at around nine. You might meet Billy, town drunk, single father who bitches about his ex-wife and how he never sees his kids.

DAVID: Fun!

RADIO: *(static)*

CALEB: What station, 950?

◌

RADIO ANNOUNCER ONE: Washington has scored on their first possession of the third quarter. 12:13 to go, 17–7, Dawgs, on the Washington Husky Sports Network.

CALEB: That's a surprise.

DAVID: That they're winning?

CALEB: That. And we get reception. Two years ago, radio and cell phone were real bad in these parts.

ANNOUNCER ONE: Joe Kruger, a much-heralded sopho-more, six-seven, 270. His older brother, Dave, played for the Baltimore Ravens. This Kruger family—outstanding defensive linemen.

ANNOUNCER TWO: And his brother Freddy, with all those movies. Figures as a slasher kind of guy. Freddy, yeah, he's over on Elm Street.

ANNOUNCER ONE: Ha ha ha. Second and ten. Huskies at their forty-eight yardline, hash on the right. Handoff to Polk: midfield, forty-five, forty, first down and then some.

○

CALEB: How often do you bump into David Downing?

DAVID: Because he's so tall and we live near each other, I see him a lot, and he always says, "Are you still writing?" I say, "Yeah." And he always says, "Well, when are you going to write another novel?" I'm like, Dude.

Caleb laughs.

DAVID: Is he just out of the loop?

CALEB: He's written four novels.

DAVID: Children's books, I think.

CALEB: Maybe, but he told me he's got four unpublished novels and is working on another. These days he's a father, edits for Amazon, likes it, gets paid well, and has time to write.

A lot of Davids: David Downing. You're David. My dad's David. David Barouh. My middle name's David.

DAVID: We'll get readers nicely confused. They'll think they're in the middle of a Faulkner novel with six people all having the same novel. I mean, the same name.

○

CALEB: I've tried all sorts of bio notes. I like the simple ones: "Caleb Powell likes hanging out with friends and family. He's always up for a beer."

DAVID: Those are good: "Anne Carson lives in Canada."

CALEB: Your bio mentions five awards you've won and that you've published eleven books and then goes on to list fifteen magazines you've written for. It's longer than the essay it's attached to. Why not just say, "David Shields can't change a flat"? Link to your blog and let that be that?

DAVID: Well.

ↄ

CALEB: You up for shooting some hoops? Then hot tub.

David picks up the ball and takes a shot, which rims out.

CALEB: You wrote about Charles Barkley and how, wherever he goes, he'd get challenged. "You work at 7-Eleven and I'm in the NBA. What makes you think I want to hoop with you?" You made him seem cool: able to hang out with the regular guy.

DAVID: *(shooting ball)* He's complicated.

CALEB: A little gimpy, but not too bad.

DAVID: I haven't shot hoops in a long time. I swim, but basketball's not good on the back.

CALEB: Okay. We'll just shoot around.

DAVID: On my way to the pool, I always walk by the Green Lake courts so I can watch a few plays, hear some funny lines. One time, I could see the ball was going to bounce directly to me, so I moved my swim bag from one side to the other and stutter-stepped in order to catch the ball in stride. I zoomed the rock behind my back to Ed Jones forty feet away. In that stentorian voice of his he just kept saying, "John Stockton! On the money! John Stockton! Dead on the money!" Highlight of my basketball life.

Caleb laughs.

DAVID: Key thing was I never looked back. Just kept walking.

○

CALEB: Classy flesh-colored shorts.

DAVID: I know. You probably thought I was naked.

CALEB: I turn around and . . . eek!

DAVID: They started out black, and I swim so much they've become brown over time.

CALEB: They went from black to brown to flesh? I'll leave the DVR right here. No splashing.

DAVID: This feels pretty damn good.

CALEB: Really nice. Check out them thar mountains.

DAVID: Don't turn it up any higher.

CALEB: It's at 104. It doesn't go any higher.

Sound of water jets turning on.

DAVID: Jets?

CALEB: We'll probably not be able to hear much. Let's take a break.

○

CALEB: *(to DVR)* October 1st, 8:09 p.m., Skykomish. Huskies win, 31–14. We're heading to the Cascadia Inn. David is driving because he wants to learn the terrain.

DAVID: Actually, because I didn't think you should be driving after—

CALEB: We've passed the train tracks at Money Creek campground and are heading to Highway 2. Take a right.

DAVID: Two lefts, then a right.

CALEB: I've got a good sense of direction because of my Oriental background.

DAVID: You're "Oriental"?

CALEB: I was born in Taiwan. I can orient. The shadows speak to the sun, the sun speaks to the shadows, and the sun and shadows speak to you.

DAVID: Town is about five miles?

CALEB: You're two feet over the white line. We're in the ditch!

DAVID: Okay. Relax. I turn here, right? I just wanted to make sure.

○

Inside the Cascadia Inn.

CALEB: Remember when we ate at Restaurant Zoe and the *amuse-bouche* came, the celery soup with crème fraîche?

DAVID: Did I make a blunder?

CALEB: You took a sip to be polite.

DAVID: I can't believe you noticed.

CALEB: Danny sent out a couple of small plates, and you wondered aloud if we'd have to pay for them. My brother-in-law is chef de cuisine and, even without a family connection, you never pay for something you didn't order.

WAITRESS: Okay, guys, have you decided?

CALEB: I'm ready.

WAITRESS: Are you ready?

DAVID: I'm ready.

WAITRESS: He's ready and you're ready. Then we're ready! All right, let's do this.

CALEB: I'll have the special. Salad, no dressing, with lemon wedges if you have them.

WAITRESS: We do.

CALEB: Awesome.

WAITRESS: How would you like your steak?

CALEB: Medium rare. And a Sierra Nevada Pale Ale.

WAITRESS: Okay. And for you? Are you together?

DAVID: Yes.

WAITRESS: *(with raised eyebrow)* Together? One bill. I can do that.

DAVID: I'll have the spaghetti with meat sauce.

WAITRESS: What kind of dressing with the salad?

DAVID: Honey mustard looks good.

WAITRESS: Honey mustard.

DAVID: And water. A pitcher of water.

WAITRESS: Alrrrrriggggght. Done deal.

CALEB: You didn't drink at all—not in high school or college?

DAVID: Very, very little.

CALEB: How many times have you been drunk in your life?

DAVID: I don't know. Depends how you define "drunk." Maybe ten times.

CALEB: I've never seen my dad drunk. He'll have the rare beer.

DAVID: I grew up in a family that didn't drink much. I drank a little in grad school, but—

WAITRESS: Here's your beer. You want a glass?

CALEB: No thanks.

DAVID: Then, somehow, from thirty to fifty, I didn't drink much at all, because it seemed to exacerbate the cystitis I had, which may be TMI. Now I'll usually have a beer with dinner. Do you find it hard to control drinking?

CALEB: Easy. When I want a beer, I'll have one. There have been times when Terry's had to pull in the reins, though. I've had moments.

○

DAVID: When Terry works from home, what does she do exactly?

CALEB: She's on the phone, answering email, talking to coworkers, preparing for presentations, going over contracts, and so on.

WAITRESS: Here it is.

CALEB: Looks great.

WAITRESS: Can I get you anything else?

DAVID: I'm good.

CALEB: One more beer.

WAITRESS: Same?

CALEB: You bet.

DAVID: She doesn't ever deal with Murdoch, does she?

CALEB: No. One degree of separation. There are 900 employees in her company, which was bought by NewsCorp, which has 50,000 employees.

DAVID: Does she feel any moral qualms about working for NewsCorp?

CALEB: Why should she?

DAVID: You don't think Murdoch is a supremely negative force in the world?

CALEB: Not only is he not a malevolent force—

DAVID: My god, are you serious?

CALEB: Completely.

DAVID: I can't believe it. What are you—a laissez-faire capitalist?

CALEB: Adam Smith was one of the great humanitarians of the eighteenth century. Pull quotes from *Wealth of Nations,* line them up with Marx or Che or Mao or even—

DAVID: Only one problem: Rupert Murdoch isn't Adam Smith.

CALEB: I'm part free market socialist, part big-government libertarian, part agnostic fundamentalist. I'm for fiscal responsibility. Socialism works for health and education; capitalism works better with restaurants and automobiles.

DAVID: Those are all easy—

CALEB: Murdoch's biases balance out the left.

DAVID: I'm not for every social program, but he tends to support extraordinarily right-wing candidates throughout the Western world. And he's hugely lowered the level of discourse in journalism and media.

CALEB: Fox News suffers from pseudo-journalism, sure.

DAVID: Even that is a very generous appraisal of what they do.

CALEB: So you're on the "crush NewsCorp" bandwagon?

DAVID: What are Terry's politics?

CALEB: She voted for Obama.

DAVID: So she's not especially conservative.

CALEB: No, but if she was, so?

DAVID: Are people at work to the right of her?

CALEB: Does it matter?

DAVID: I thought you were the person who thought politics mattered.

CALEB: She works with highly ethical and motivated people for a company that treats their employees well.

DAVID: Huh?

CALEB: You question life and death, but don't question your own views about Rupert Murdoch?

DAVID: And you've suddenly lowered your periscope to whether a company gives its employees three-week vacations?

WAITRESS: Is anything the matter?

CALEB: The beer?

WAITRESS: Here's your beer.

CALEB: Thanks much. What was I saying? People on the right aren't "evil." Rupert Murdoch isn't "evil." Terry's been treated fairly; her coworkers are treated fairly; they have good benefits. The harder you work, the more you get paid. NewsCorp gives more than they have to in benefits and vacations, and they recognized gay unions when they didn't have to. NewsCorp owns HarperCollins, for crying out loud. Does Barbara Kingsolver have "moral qualms" about cashing her HarperCollins royalty check? Do Matt Groening and *The Simpsons* posse, guys like Harry Shearer, have "moral qualms" that NewsCorp makes them multimillionaires? You must have really liked your food.

DAVID: It's delicious. The food is really good here.

CALEB: It hits the spot.

◌

CALEB: Sam Harris, in *The Moral Landscape,* says that psychopaths represent one percent of the population. Martha Stout, in *The Sociopath Next Door,* says they represent four percent of the population. Someone's wrong.

DAVID: I'd vote for four.

CALEB: Take Milgram, add human history and moral absolutes, and you can make a case that we're all sociopaths.

DAVID: I'm not. I recognize the reality of other human beings.

CALEB: Depends. My aunt Grace, a poet and my mom's sister, wrote a poem about the death of her cat. And the point of her poem was that people die all the time everywhere, but she didn't care. She was devastated by the death of her cat. Grace is a warm, caring person. Of course she's not a sociopath, but—

DAVID: I don't see how it illustrates your point. A sociopath acts on his antisocial sentiments. He is incapable of empathy or remorse. Your aunt just misses her cat. They're not remotely the same thing.

CALEB: I'm trying to get to John Donne: "Any man's death

diminishes me, because I am involved in mankind." Are we diminished? Are we involved? I'm working off what you said about Bush. It comes down to how many points of separation there are between you and responsibility. You thought George Bush evil. You more or less accused him of being a sociopath. Not to mention Rupert Murdoch and Fox News. Therefore, I could make a somewhat exaggerated yet plausible case that you see a world divided, half full of sociopaths responsible for, say, collateral damage in Iraq but sans remorse or empathy or responsibility. I'm playing devil's advocate, of course, and using rhetorical—

DAVID: Wait, this is all just a devil's advocate argument for you?

WAITRESS: Apple pie?

DAVID: Sounds great. Do you have ice cream?

WAITRESS: You bet. All right, apple pie it is.

CALEB: The "survivor" episode of *Curb [Your Enthusiasm]*: The rabbi asks Larry, "Hey, a good friend of mine is a survivor. Could I bring him?" Larry says sure. Larry's father's friend, Solly, is also a survivor. Solly is ninety, has a glass eye, "very Jewish." Solly shows up and says, "Where's the survivor?" The rabbi brings out this young guy. Solly goes, "You're not a survivor." And the guy goes, "I am, too, a survivor. Survivor Australia, ten days without shoes, poisonous snakes." Solly says, "Holocaust, one loaf of bread a week, ten degrees below, Poland."

DAVID: You want to share?

CALEB: I'll have a bite.

○

DAVID: Ian Hamilton was a British biographer and editor. A friend came up to him and said, "You know, all this drinking we always do—I'm not sure I really even enjoy it anymore." Hamilton said, "Enjoy it? Whoever said you were supposed to enjoy it?" I love that line. It's a very British way of saying no matter what you do you're fucked.

CALEB: You love to say that, that we're fucked. "We die and so therefore we're fucked." That's your thing. You and I aren't that fucked.

DAVID: We're back now to the Khmer Rouge?

Silence.

DAVID: But the drinking, I mean. Do you get pretty lit at these social—

CALEB: Like tonight, you mean? . . . Remember when some politician said corporations are people?

DAVID: Romney.

CALEB: Corporations *are* people. Microsoft employs ninety thousand.

DAVID: Corporations are populated by millionaires.

CALEB: Would you rather live in a country with corporations and millionaires? I've been to places without either. They suck.

DAVID: I see your point, but corporations have been given—

CALEB: Capitalism is two restaurants in a place that can support only one. The restaurant that provides the freshest, tastiest food for the best price and with the best service will survive, and the restaurant that serves crap will die. And that's how it should be.

DAVID: No one's arguing for the end of capitalism. Even Norman Goldman.

CALEB: Yeah, well, Goldman and Limbaugh cancel one another out.

DAVID: Hardly.

CALEB: Both are wrong.

DAVID: You actually go out of your way to listen to talk radio?

CALEB: I'm in the car at least an hour a day, taking the girls to school, to day care, going to the health club, running errands, and that's all I listen to.

DAVID: What do the kids want?

CALEB: Music. I'm a dictator when I drive. As they get older, they'll make more noise.

DAVID: I promise you, you won't be listening to talk radio anymore.

CALEB: They already have "princess" disease.

DAVID: In the sense of wanting to dress up as princesses?

CALEB: In the form of wanting to be treated like princesses.

DAVID: Those three girls are pretty cute.

CALEB: We went to Disneyland. I call the experience the closest I've ever been face-to-face with evil. They could get rid of Guantánamo and make terrorists spend a day in Disneyland—they'd talk.

DAVID: It was pretty painful? The one in LA?

CALEB: Doors open at ten a.m. We get there a little before, and I'm surprised: the line's not so bad. Terry's pregnant with Kaya. Ava's almost four and Gia's two. Two and under are free, but we still pay two hundred bucks for two adults and a kid. That's a living monthly wage in Thailand. We go in to Disney Village: mountains and oceans of people. The gates to Disneyland won't open until eleven. We have two kids dying for Disneyland, and they want every toy they see in every store. Mickey Mouse puzzle: eighteen bucks. Lion King figure: six bucks. We die a slow death for one hour. Eleven a.m. approaches, people line up, the girls are going nuts, we finally get in at maybe quarter after eleven, and every ride is jammed. We start at the Snow White adventure, wait fifteen minutes, sit down for the ride, and then we come out and keep doing it for another eight hours. Line, ride, line, ride, line, ride, we get done, and Terry turns to me and says, "That was fun. Let's come back tomorrow!"

DAVID: Ouch.

CALEB: You never went? You didn't take Natalie to Disneyland?

DAVID: Almost, once.

CALEB: Did Natalie want to go?

DAVID: I was up for it. I'd put on my anthropological pith helmet and try to — wasn't it fascinating?

CALEB: It's an odd study of the human animal. We had lunch at the Rain Forest Café (cruddy food at high prices), but they had beer. Terry says, "You get a beer. The kids are having a great time. It's not so bad, is it?"

○

Back at Khamta's house.

CALEB: The opening of *Still Life with Woodpecker*: "Albert

Camus wrote that the only serious question is whether to kill yourself or not." Tom Robbins then says, "There *is* only one serious question. And that is: *Who knows how to make love stay?* Answer me that and I will tell you whether or not to kill yourself."

DAVID: "Who knows how to make love stay?"

CALEB: That gets to something.

DAVID: No, it doesn't. That takes Camus and turns him into Rod McKuen. That's terrible.

CALEB: The Robbins line reminds me of William Gass's "Politics . . . for all those not in love." Both are getting to the same place.

DAVID: The only reason Robbins is a romantic is he's bedded more women than Sinatra.

CALEB: I partly agree with you about Robbins. Too many talking spoons.

DAVID: *(strumming the guitar)* I'd now like to sing some songs I've written.

CALEB: You're a musician?

DAVID: No. I wish.

CALEB: There's a comedian inside you dying to escape.

DAVID: Oh, he's escaped.

○

CALEB: You know, when you read my first novel, for class, you compared it to *The Stranger*. My narrator describes childhood, going to Sunday school, and a teacher tells him, "In heaven, when you fall, an angel will catch you." I close the paragraph by saying, "My childhood must have been wonderful." And you compared this detachment, I had thought positively, to Camus: "Mother died today, or maybe it was yesterday."

DAVID: I did mean it as praise, but compared to *The Fall*, *The Stranger* is a slog.

CALEB: I love when the warden shows Meursault the cross and tells him that every prisoner, before execution, breaks down and weeps. Meursault calls bullshit, sending the warden into a rage. Meursault's a sociopath, incapable of feeling guilt or joy in the lives of others, indifferent and malleable, willing to go along with his surroundings. The novel satisfies my X factor.

DAVID: To me, it's all so obvious what Camus is doing and saying in *The Stranger*. You get it on about page twelve. I've tried to teach *The Fall* many times, and most students hate it. They literally throw the book across the room. Maybe it's a limitation of my aesthetic: basically, the only thing I really love is listening to people think really well about existence for 120 pages. What else is worth my time?

It's the same argument we had about your Polynesian transvestite story. You thought that by laying in all these images and motifs you're building all this power, but you're not, at least to me. You need to get in there and wrestle with the material much more overtly, have the narrator think aloud about everything, not just move from scene to scene.

CALEB: *The Stranger* ends: ". . . they shall greet me with howls of execration." In another translation the title is *The Outsider*, and it ends with "cries of hatred."

DAVID: That's terrible.

CALEB: It's a more literal translation of *"cris de haine."*

DAVID: "Howls of execration" is so beautiful.

○

CALEB: For the *Nervous Breakdown*, I wrote a comparison: "Tao Lin's *Richard Yates* vs. the 2006 Dodge Caravan Owner's Manual."

DAVID: Do you own one?

CALEB: Terry does. The manual kicks Tao Lin's ass.

DAVID: Maybe envy is a young man's disease. Of course I want my work to be admired—be as famous to the world as I am to myself, as a teacher of mine (the same woman who told me the Toni Morrison anecdote) once said—but I'm so busy I literally don't have time for it. The title essay of a book Stanley Crouch wrote was a lengthy critique of *Black Planet*: he thought I needed to write more about being a Jew in America, or something like that. He got [David's former UW colleague] Charles Johnson to keep faxing me things to try to get my dander up, but I didn't have any interest. That book was years in the past by then.

This may be self-glorifying on my part, but do you feel any envy toward me or my work?

CALEB: I'm a nobody. I've got nothing. I'd like to take the high road, though, and say that I don't. How am I diminished by the success of others? When I was single, did it bother me that other men dated fantastic women? When I played basketball with Nate Robinson or Jamal Crawford [NBA players who grew up in Seattle] or played music with fantastic musicians, I was aware of my inferiority. I want to be better, but I like the challenge. Being on the same court or stage improved my skills. I'd rather be the worst player on the court; my own game will rise. Reading high-intellect writing has the same effect. I did get a kick out of Eric Lundgren's two-star review of *Reality Hunger* on Amazon.

DAVID: Let's pull back and look at the thing from afar: What are we doing here over this long weekend? Are you in some sense seeking validation, approval, manuscript appraisal, career counseling? I'm seeking in a way the opposite. I'm seeing if you can undermine me, so I can restart my engine. Feel free to offer devastating or semi-devastating critiques of me and/or my work.

CALEB: If you're looking for a critique, *Remote* is probably my least favorite.

DAVID: Ooh, really? I still like that book a lot.

CALEB: What else? The Spider-Man thing in *How Literature Saved My Life* and the chapter in *Reality Hunger* when you do little responses to other people's books. Your collage books read like *Esquire*'s "Dubious Achievements."

DAVID: I gotta stop you. That is so ridiculous.

CALEB: Good bathroom reading, doctor's office reading.

DAVID: Ha ha.

CALEB: What you consider velocity means quickly skip one paragraph for the next; it lacks the feeling of being in a book. A good novel gets progressively more interesting. Your books lack this momentum and acceleration; the first ten pages are as good as the last ten. To you, there may be structure, but you could almost read *Reality Hunger* backward and get the same impression.

DAVID: I don't know what to say. You don't have a clue how to read my work.

○

CALEB: Here's your letter, dated January 4, 1993, complete with a six-digit number so I can't call you back.

DAVID: What an idiot!

Dear Caleb,

Happy New Year's greetings from your former creative writing teacher. How are you doing? I hope you're still writing. The novel you were working on in class a couple years ago showed a lot of potential. To me, the strongest section of the novel dealt with your protagonist on Capitol Hill; by emphasizing that material, you could produce a very effective coming-of-age novel.

"I walked out of the kitchen and went outside. There they were—the stars, the moon, the gentle hum of the sea, and the black paper cut-outs of the trees against the night; there they were." Are these lines from your book? Do I have the lines right? Is there any chance I could use (beg, borrow, or steal) these lines in my own work-in-progress, a strange mix of fiction, nonfiction, and autobiography about mass media?

All best,

David Shields

Phone: 548-363

○

CALEB: In many ways, my asking you for help opened up our relationship.

DAVID: Probably so.

CALEB: If I hadn't asked for a blurb, and then hadn't called you a dork, who knows?

DAVID: Yeah—who knows?

CALEB: I'd rather be insulted and dismissed by a genius than flattered by an idiot. I'm by no means saying you're a genius, but you're very critical of my work.

DAVID: Not particularly.

CALEB: You've never been blown away by anything I've written. It's not as if my goal in life is to blow David Shields away, but any writer wants to impress the reader. I've sent you various things, unpublished, published, and you've never been knocked out. Even my collage of eighteen genocidal deaths, you said, "Ehh."

○

CALEB: A lot of today's artists lack experience. They're not in a prison, but they're sheltered. They're David Markson holed up in his New York City apartment, Tao Lin and Blake Butler at their computers, David Shields in academia. Do you know Chekhov's "The Bet"?

David shakes his head.

CALEB: Two men argue over what's harder to endure, life in prison or the death penalty. The banker believes life in prison to be a slow, cruel death, while the young lawyer thinks prison isn't so bad, and thus death would be worse. The banker challenges the lawyer, and they bet whether the lawyer can survive solitary confinement for fifteen years. There are conditions: the lawyer can have a piano, books, wine, and so forth. The lawyer lives fifteen years in solitary confinement, but by this time the banker is no longer wealthy and can't pay. The lawyer, though, has tasted the fragrance of life through literature. He writes a note saying he doesn't want the money, and disappears to roam the earth. The banker locks the note away.

DAVID: Either you told it badly or once again Chekhov does precious little for me. I don't get it.

CALEB: The point seems to be that life experienced through the prism of art trumps the experience of life.

DAVID: Sign me up for that.

CALEB: Who said you could journey around the world in the comfort of your library?

DAVID: Let me intercede. I do think it's a continuum. Somehow we wind up portraying you as a man of vast experience and me as someone locked away in a nunnery, but—and this is really sad to have to say—but I've lived a full life. I've married, raised a child, traveled, taught, stuttered.

CALEB: *(laughing)* I agree. I think it's possible to live life at ground level and never leave a five-mile radius.

DAVID: You do? Good, because that's pretty much what Kierkegaard—

CALEB: Not really. No.

○

DAVID: Don't you think, contrariwise, that you've erred, that you've indulged in life too much, that you've devoted yourself insufficiently to art? You've been too eager to accumulate experience for experience's sake.

CALEB: I've procrastinated. I've failed. I've overestimated my abilities and underestimated the difficulties.

DAVID: You probably thought, Hey, I'm going to have fun and then I'll be able to turn it on. It probably wasn't crucial to you, whereas it was everything to me to become a writer. I had to become a writer.

CALEB: In high school I wanted to be a jock. In college I became a dedicated writer, temporarily. Afterward, I wanted to be a musician. Then it was travel and language. I figured all this would help my writing.

DAVID: It has. You have a range of reference I couldn't pretend to match.

CALEB: I regressed. My form got all messed up. After studying Korean and Chinese, you learn to think without articles, so I tried writing without articles: "He went inside room, saw woman cry, sat, picked up bottle, drank beer." I wrote my rape novel like this; I thought I was being revolutionary to say everything in literally as few words as possible. Minimalist, different. I gave early chapters to a few friends, and they couldn't stand it. Still, experience hasn't been a waste, and I never stopped reading. If anything, I read more overseas. I'm drafting and setting stories in Taiwan, Brazil, Thailand, Korea, Hong Kong, the UAE.

DAVID: Isaiah Berlin's hedgehog and the fox. You're the fox: you know many things. I'm the hedgehog: I know one thing.

○

CALEB: When I lived in Al Ain, a small city in the emirate of Abu Dhabi, two Pakistani cabdrivers were publicly executed.

DAVID: Did you see it?

CALEB: I didn't know about it until after. Some of my high school students had. They told me about it.

DAVID: Why'd they execute the cabdrivers—took the long way to the airport?

CALEB: They murdered fares and dumped the corpses in the desert. Over 20,000 people attended. The two were tied to these posts and publicly humiliated for their last twenty-four hours. They were cordoned off. People would walk up to them, two feet away, and spit or curse or whatever. It was September and over a hundred degrees; they gave them just enough water to keep them alive, maximize suffering for twenty-four hours. Then they were shot.

DAVID: Ford Madox Ford says if you have any imagination at all, the death of a mouse by cancer is the whole sack of Rome by the Goths. Flannery O'Connor said any good writer has plenty of material for the rest of her life if she survived childhood.

CALEB: You think too much about literature.

○

CALEB: In your writing you seem very conscious of Jewish identity. I never considered myself Jewish. My parents only reminded me that it was in my blood.

DAVID: I'd had no idea you were a quarter Jewish, but I can see you now as a Talmudic scholar.

CALEB: My dad's cousin lives in Los Angeles: Jerry Benezra, a union lawyer.

DAVID: He's probably best friends with my half brother, who lives in LA.

CALEB: I grew up, basically, Christian. My parents aren't very religious, but they thought church was the right thing to do, so we went. They stopped when I was about twelve.

DAVID: Does your dad view himself as Jewish?

CALEB: No. And he went to Jewish school until he was nine.

DAVID: Is he anti-Semitic?

CALEB: Not at all. I'd even say he's hard-line pro-Israeli.

DAVID: What about your mom?

CALEB: Same. Pro-Israeli. Her dad was anti-Semitic, though. His name was James Edmond Wilson. Initials: J.E.W. He didn't like that, said racist things at home. She ended up marrying a man who was half-Jewish.

David laughs.

CALEB: He was a superior court judge: The Honorary James Wilson. He molested some of his daughters, my aunts. They went to my grandmother and wanted her to go to the police. Grandma Betty didn't.

DAVID: How does anyone do that?

CALEB: It's unimaginable. My grandmother protected my grandfather. My mother didn't go to the funeral of either of her parents.

DAVID: Was she molested?

CALEB: If she was, she would never say. It's murky; she claims he did something to them but not to her, though he didn't molest them all. We, meaning my sisters and I, have debated how screwed up my mother's family was. My mother was the oldest of six children—five girls. This we know: of the five girls, the third and fourth oldest were molested and made a fuss, warned the youngest, and protected her. Locked doors.

DAVID: That is a weird fucking impulse. You have three daughters, I have one, and I could no more molest Natalie than—

CALEB: I don't know any of my aunts, except one: she's the San Francisco poet, Aunt Grace, and she was one of the two who were molested; hers is a real-life version of distorted memory. Grace's stories change depending on the listener. She has talked to Terry, my sisters, me, and told the horror story: Grandpa was a pedophile. But even Grace doesn't want to tarnish the family name. It's not my pain to own.

DAVID: My advice to J.E.W. would have been, "Just go to a prostitute and dress her up in pigtails if you need to."

○

DAVID: There was this beautiful thing in the *New Yorker* recently by Joan Acocella about the novelist Paula Fox, who is Courtney Love's grandma, believe it or not. Fox grew up with a very cold mother who had five abortions, didn't want Paula, was inordinately neglectful. Acocella argues through Fox that when people grow up in an emotionally barren landscape, they tend to (1) become passive, (2) think of themselves as not being sure of their feelings and/or not sure they have feelings, and (3) if they're writers, get their revenge by not forgetting a thing and analyzing everyone, including themselves, in a harsh light.

CALEB: You identify.

DAVID: You might say.

CALEB: It sounds like you didn't have much "like," not to mention "love." Between you and your sister, your mother, there may have been love, but there wasn't warmth.

DAVID: My father was severely manic-depressive, in and out of mental hospitals his entire life, and my mother was extremely autocratic. Did you grow up in a much more nourishing family? You definitely felt loved?

CALEB: My mom was happy and enthusiastic but lazy— a horrible cook.

DAVID: How would you know she loved you?

CALEB: She told us all the time. She'd go to my sports games and howl my name every time I came to bat. She smothered.

DAVID: Your mother hugged you?

CALEB: You saw her. She gave you a hug.

DAVID: Was she affectionate?

CALEB: She smothered us, but she didn't do the heavy lifting.

DAVID: How about your dad?

CALEB: Humorless and boring. Strict. By the book.

DAVID: He's mellowed a little, though?

CALEB: He's aged well. More easygoing.

DAVID: Your daughters softened him.

CALEB: He plays "pease, porridge, hot" with them, takes them to parks. I don't remember him smiling nearly this much when I was a kid. I never faced the coldness you seem to remember from your parents, though. Sure, growing up, I was left to myself. We didn't do much as a family. I had my friends Mark and Vince, for example, and they had much more influence. But I had two stable parents who loved each other, loved their children, and this was their sole purpose and meaning in life.

DAVID: Wow. That's a lot.

CALEB: My dad was my Little League coach. He likes baseball but never played. He was at the game Bobby Thomson hit the "shot heard round the world."

DAVID: He better have been pulling for the Dodgers.

CALEB: Big Brooklyn Dodgers fan, like your dad. He always kept score, so he had the scorecard of the "shot heard round the world" game. He was in the outfield, upper level, and the ball went out of view, so he could tell it was a home run only by the reaction of the crowd. When he went to Vietnam, he put the scorecard in his mom's attic. She threw it out. In good condition, it would be worth $100,000 now.

DAVID: He should have kept it in a glass case.

CALEB: Knowing my dad, he probably did.

DAVID: What does he think life's about? Does he ever show a spark? What are his passions?

CALEB: He thinks the same way about everything as he did fifty years ago. He was a captain in the navy; the next change of command would have made him an admiral, but he says he lacked the necessary political savvy, so after thirty years he retired. They have only one TV, no cable, and the TV is used only for movies. He and my mom rate movies, from one to ten—every movie they've ever watched. For my dad, movies must have a happy ending. Period.

○

CALEB: My mother always covered for me. Once she kept a few speeding tickets from my father. The insurance company raised family rates exorbitantly high, and my dad found out. He wasn't happy.

DAVID: Did he yell?

CALEB: He did.

DAVID: What would he say "Goddamnit, Caleb, I can't believe you did this!"?

CALEB: He doesn't swear.

DAVID: What did he say?

CALEB: "How could you lie, Trice—why? Of all the stupid things, to let that son of ours keep driving!" My dad's nerdy. He rarely gets angry these days.

DAVID: I hope Natalie has children, because I think I'd be a good grandparent. I would love to have grandkids and get to be silly again. It would be fun.

CALEB: I hope that happens.

DAVID: The girls must be so fun for your parents.

CALEB: Whenever I give them a treat—say, ice cream—they all sit down with big eyes, and I give them a chocolate-chip-size dollop.

DAVID: The tiniest bit?

CALEB: A pinprick of ice cream.

DAVID: Each time?

CALEB: The joke never gets old. They get the bowls, look with sad eyes, and say, "No, Daddy." I ham it up for as long as I can, and then I give them a regular-size portion. One time Terry asked the kids who's funnier, and they said, "Dad!" She asked, "Why?" And they said, "Because he always gives us small ice cream."

DAVID: Darling.

CALEB: Grandkids would be fun.

○

CALEB: Your mom died a long time ago, right?

DAVID: 1977.

CALEB: When you were an aspiring writer.

DAVID: I was twenty and just starting to publish in my college magazine, similar to the point you were when you were in my class.

CALEB: Would she have been happy?

DAVID: I sometimes think I've spent the last thirty-five years trying to make my dead mother proud of me.

CALEB: Your dad seemed more ambivalent.

DAVID: When he was around me, he was always incredibly competitive and reluctant to offer praise of any kind. When he was with other people, he talked endlessly about me, apparently. I think of him as a Zen genius in reverse: wherever he was, he wasn't.

○

CALEB: "But the less commercially viable fiction became, the less it seemed to concern itself with its audience, which in turn made it less commercial, until, like a dying star, it seems on the verge of implosion. Indeed, most American writers seem to have forgotten how to write about big issues—as if giving two shits about the world has gotten crushed under the boot sole—"

DAVID: "Brute soul"?

CALEB: "Boot sole." Like a shoe. ". . . boot sole of postmodernism. At the same time, young writers will have to swear off navel-gazing in favor of an outward glance onto a wrecked and lovely world worthy and in need of the attention of intelligent, sensitive writers. I'm saying that writers need to venture out from under the protective wing of academia, to put themselves and their work on the line."

DAVID: Who are you quoting?

CALEB: Ted Genoways, editor of the *Virginia Quarterly Review.*

DAVID: It's just a regurgitation of the Tom Wolfe argument that we're all supposed to write about . . . wait—are we out of batteries?

DAY 4

CALEB: *(to DVR)* October 2nd, 2011, Skykomish, Washington. Last day of the trip. Nothing like a sober rant first thing in the morning. Two things piss me off: Cruel and unusual punishment is a tautology. Cruel, to me, is releasing a rapist-murderer into society after he "pays his debt" because that shows cruelty toward the victim. What's cruel? Manson's victims' relatives having to endlessly appear at parole hearings because the law grants Manson the possibility of being set free.

Second, I think drugs, prostitution, gambling—all these so-called vices—should be legal but regulated and controlled. And if you commit crimes when using, rather than it being a mitigating factor, it should be aggravating.

DAVID: Good luck getting that one through.

CALEB: Did you put the sugar and other stuff back over here? Oh, I see. Garbage is right there. . . . The thing you realize with drugs is, there's a cost. I stopped smoking pot at nineteen. And with other drugs, after you do them, you don't need to do them. I mean, an altered state can be fun, but drugs have a detrimental effect. Long- and short-term.

DAVID: How much acid have you done?

CALEB: Maybe a half dozen times.

DAVID: Huh. I would have thought maybe more. You're definitely a brother from another planet.

CALEB: Did you put the milk over there?

DAVID: Over here.

CALEB: I'm no doctor, but I've heard that organs and tissue can regenerate when young: smokers who stop at thirty can have almost full recovery—

DAVID: That's when Laurie stopped smoking. We hope and assume—

CALEB: At fifty the lungs get only so much back, and at seventy or eighty they will never regenerate. That's how it works with the brain. When I took acid, I could feel this searing inside my head. Acid isn't addictive, but it was obvious it could make you crazy.

○

DAVID: I love what the comedian Rick Reynolds says about the Bible: "Great story. Wish I could believe it."

CALEB: You ever read *Barabbas*?

DAVID: The Marlowe play?

CALEB: The Pär Lagerkvist novel.

DAVID: It was originally a Christopher Marlowe play. Barabbas goes back to the Bible.

CALEB: Lagerkvist was familiar with the play, but Marlowe's Barabbas is a sociopath, full of rage, an unrepentant killer. Lagerkvist's Barabbas comes across as searching and humble.

DAVID: I'm Lagerkvist's Barabbas. You're more—

CALEB: Not funny.

◌

CALEB: Let's bring out the riding lawn mower. Time for a morning beer.

DAVID: Beer?

CALEB: Shakespeare: "Every morning just before breakfast, I don't want no coffee or tea. / It's just me and my good Buddy Weiser, that's all I ever need."

DAVID: Shakespeare?

CALEB: A lesser-known character: The Duke of Thorogood. Can't mow without beer—you want one?

DAVID: No thanks.

◌

They depart from Khamta's house for a short walk in the woods before leaving.

DAVID: That was fun. I've never driven a lawn mower. So we hike, go back, have lunch, and maybe we can watch the Seahawks game somewhere, but I need to be back in time for Natalie's call. I can't miss that.

CALEB: You bet. Even though you claim *Heroes* is your mediocre first novel published thirty years ago and is invented "whole cloth," it takes from your knowledge of life, which isn't invented. Your personality controls every word. In some ways it's more you than anything you've written. It says a lot about you: What sort of man are you? What is your morality? What sort of husband would you become, what sort of father? The idea that the main character would cheat and feel guilt, feel overburdened with a diabetic son, worry about being an inadequate parent—of everything you've written, *Heroes* most accurately predicts your apprehension of fatherhood, marriage, and not wanting a second child. I could argue it's your most autobiographical book.

DAVID: And I could argue *This Seething Ocean, That Damned Eagle* is a brilliant title.

○

DAVID: Through my early thirties, against a lackadaisical defender, I could look like a genius on the basketball court, but the moment someone stronger and quicker D'd-up against me, I would completely vanish.

CALEB: It's part mental: just get the shot off.

DAVID: But it's also physical. It's real. If he's hand-checking you, you have to be able to put the ball on the ground and take it to the hoop. And I couldn't.

○

Nearing the end of a road completely washed out by a flood.

CALEB: Let's check out the washed-out bridge.

DAVID: Can we really just walk over it like this?

CALEB: Interesting, how the river veered here and swept the earth out from underneath the road.

DAVID: How could the water wash out the road? That would have to be an awfully strong current.

CALEB: Maybe heavy rains and ice pack melt, and it all came rushing down the mountain. Let me take a picture.

DAVID: Jump in the water, take a little swim.

CALEB: Freeze to death for dramatic purposes?

○

CALEB: Kosinski's *Steps*—good stuff, no argument—but *The Painted Bird* provokes thought and leaves the reader alone.

DAVID: I don't want to be left alone.

○

They walk down a dirt road toward a vacant monastery.

DAVID: I love in *The Ambassadors* when Strether says, "Live all you can; it's a mistake not to. It doesn't so much matter what you do in particular so long as you have your life. If you haven't had that what *have* you had?" It's easy for Henry James to write that toward the end of his life. He'd devoted himself entirely to art.

CALEB: Maugham said James wrote as if there were a lively

cocktail party next door, but the voices were too far away to hear, and the fence was too tall to peer over.

DAVID: To Maugham, that was probably a criticism, but to me that's what makes James great. Life feels like that to anyone who's a serious artist.

CALEB: That's not really life.

DAVID: I remember once, toward the end of high school, I performed some chore incompetently—vacuum my room, I forget what—and when I romanticized my incompetence, my mother said, "Just because you're a 'writer' doesn't mean you have to be a schlemiel." Laurie and I met at an artists' colony outside Chicago called Ragdale, where her job was to fix stuff and make dinners. And now sometimes, when she's a little drunk, she'll say, "You just married me so I'd take care of you."

Caleb laughs.

DAVID: You wanted to become an artist, but you overcommitted to life. I wanted to become a human being, but I overcommitted . . . Oh my god . . .

CALEB: The crematorium.

DAVID: It's not Tibetan, is it?

CALEB: Chinese characters. 山寺: mountain temple.

DAVID: Only the chimney remains.

CALEB: A few years ago people used these grounds. The monastery must have been lovely. The deck doesn't seem so solid. We could fall through.

DAVID: That would be totally schlemiel.

CALEB: Still life: *David Shields in pond.*

DAVID: Wonder if they'll ever rebuild.

CALEB: I stayed at a monastery in the backwaters of Thailand. You want to contemplate eternity and suffering and the ten Buddhist precepts—hang out at a monastery.

DAVID: Are you and Terry equally competent?

CALEB: She seems to think she's more competent, and I agree. I'm the schlemiel.

DAVID: You're still the artist figure, even though you take care of the kids?

CALEB: We've got a good balance. I don't know about opposites. There's no such thing. The opposite of "artsy" isn't practical or businesslike or mathematical.

DAVID: There is a yin and a yang. I do think that Laurie and I are more different than some couples are. Some people marry others who are quite similar to themselves, and I always thought I would, and to my surprise and delight, I didn't.

CALEB: There's almost more friction between artists. What if your wife wrote ultra-conventional novels?

David laughs.

CALEB: I had a musician friend who dated a singer. She had all this musical equipment, microphone, sound systems, but she had no talent. My friend said he couldn't go forward in a relationship with someone who was so blind to her own faults.

Even two artists who love the same form might clash. One could be a messy night owl, the other tidy and an early bird. One's vegetarian and one isn't. One drinks too much; the other hates drinking.

DAVID: To be very honest, in previous relationships with

either writers or visual artists, they would look to me to take care of them. I was supposed to be the strong, silent, competent, sane one. My reaction was always, You're not serious—you want me to be the rational one? No, I get to be the overanxious artist. A composer named David Del Tredici once said to me, "One Jesus child per family."

○

They walk down another forest service road.

CALEB: I'm going to get them to take a picture of us.

DAVID: Do you know them?

CALEB: No. *(to a couple on their front lawn)* How you doin'?

WOMAN: Great.

CALEB: Could you do us a favor?

WOMAN: Sure.

CALEB: Take three or four. Click here.

WOMAN: Do you want a close-up or far away?

CALEB: Where we are will be fine. Great. Thanks.

MAN: Where you guys off to?

CALEB: Just taking a walk. I'm a journalist, and this guy I'm with is from out of state. Witness protection. His memoir is coming out—under a pseudonym, of course.

David laughs quietly.

CALEB: Seriously.

WOMAN: Can we read about it?

CALEB: *Seattle Times* will have a piece out in about six months, timed to coincide with the book's release.

○

Sound of steps on gravel.

CALEB: Okay, let's talk about your past in the mob.

DAVID: Bugsy Malone and I were like this.

CALEB: Sunglasses, the black jacket, bald head. You kept silent, didn't give anything away with your high-pitched voice.

DAVID: I don't think they bought it.

CALEB: Probably not.

DAVID: What do you think they're doing—just cleaning up their yard?

CALEB: Kill two birds: clear out yard, stack firewood for the winter. I should have thought of a nickname for you.

DAVID: If I were really in witness protection, you wouldn't have said that.

CALEB: True.

DAVID: Did you make all of that up on the spot?

CALEB: Not very good improv.

DAVID: Not bad.

CALEB: *Skykomish Witch Project.*

DAVID: I don't think that's our title, but I can see it being a line in the book. It's really turned out interesting, hasn't it? When we left, on Thursday evening, I was thinking it's perfectly possible we would come up empty.

CALEB: I thought, Who knows? Maybe it'll be more of a writers' retreat than any big conversation. We'd get time to read and relax, but we didn't—

DAVID: Don't you think we got what we wanted?

CALEB: We've covered most of my concerns. My beefs are not so much with you as with artists in general. Writers today don't concern themselves with powerful and important topics. And I got to find out about you, see you in a different way.

DAVID: How so?

CALEB: Warmer. More friendly. Earlier you said there isn't a pretentious bone in your body, and now I see what you mean.

DAVID: That's a nice thing to say. Thanks.

CALEB: This is where you say something good about me.

DAVID: I knew you were smart, but I had no idea you were this smart.

○

CALEB: Some things, unfortunately or not, have to stay out of the final draft.

DAVID: We pushed limits.

CALEB: We can't betray everyone.

DAVID: We can't?

CALEB: We went as far as we could.

DAVID: Some of our secrets need to stay secret.

CALEB: You agree?

DAVID: I guess.

○

Back at the house, preparing to leave.

DAVID: Obviously, I'm a sugar fiend. This is probably going to sound kind of weird, but one of the issues between us is control vs. loss of control: Apollonian vs. Dionysian. I'm a very moderate drinker. Only in the last couple of years have I even started to drink at all, although I now dearly love my bottle of Pike Kilt Lifter Ruby Ale every night. "Let the healing begin." I don't know how to judge drinking, is what I'm trying to say. And I don't know how much you drank this morning. But I'm not totally comfortable with you driving us home.

CALEB: Ah.

DAVID: So I thought I would drive. But also, I wonder—do you not have any drinking issues? Am I totally misreading that? I'm such a nondrinker, but I thought if you drink heavily before lunch, isn't that supposedly a sign? Tell me if I'm totally off base.

CALEB: Terry notices.

DAVID: You seem like a great guy, but you've had three or four beers before lunch, and perhaps the weekend is, for you, a wonderful time to unwind or whatever. I'm just raising it as a boring Safety Patrol thing: Do you want me to drive? Secondarily, friend to friend, do you think you have your drinking under control, or is it a slight issue? A nonissue? Tell me your thoughts.

CALEB: If this were coming from Terry I'd say—

DAVID: "Fuck you?"

CALEB: Well, no, I'd try to put on a legitimate defense. I woke up at seven thirty and had a beer when I mowed the lawn. I put a beer in the cup holder and took off. And then I had a couple more as we cleaned up. One more after the hike. And I always tell Terry that a beer an hour—

DAVID: Is a fun buzz.

CALEB: She told me once, "I'll always remember our honeymoon in Belize. It was the first time I counted beers, and one day I counted twelve." Sometimes, if we barbecue into evening and I've had eight beers, she'll say, "Caleb, you've had eight beers." And I'll say, "It's been eight hours." I think I'm fine to drive.

DAVID: Okay, but your speech has gotten—

CALEB: Am I slurring?

DAVID: A lot.

CALEB: Okay.

DAVID: Again, Laurie makes fun of me, because if anyone drinks much at all, I always think they're roaring alcoholics.

CALEB: And with my past . . .

DAVID: Transvestites, car accidents, last night, the night before . . .

CALEB: I've never had a DUI, never had an arrest or problem.

DAVID: How is it in your life in general?

CALEB: Terry says don't drink before five p.m.

DAVID: Right.

CALEB: Sometimes, you know, I'll have a beer before that, but I feel you.

DAVID: I love how they say that in *The Wire*: "I feel you." I'm not in any way judging it.

CALEB: You should judge.

DAVID: I'm not.

CALEB: You're raising it.

DAVID: I'm just saying, practically, do you want me to drive?

For instance, if you want to drink during lunch, cool. I'll drive.

CALEB: I see why you wanted to drive to the Cascadia last night.

DAVID: The irony being you're probably a better driver drunk than I am sober.

CALEB: I was freaking!

DAVID: I was driving super slow.

CALEB: Whenever a car came the other way, your right tire went well over the white line and onto the shoulder.

DAVID: But there wasn't any harm over there, was there?

CALEB: No.

DAVID: I'm definitely a cautious driver. A granny driver. I just thought I'd bring it up.

CALEB: I'm not an angry drunk. A foolish one, perhaps. On vacation in Mexico I'm able to maintain a buzz. You drink two beers quickly, you have a buzz, and then, for me, if I drink too much it becomes unpleasant.

DAVID: Don't you need food in your system?

CALEB: That matters. If I'm going too far, I drink a seltzer.

DAVID: You do moderate it.

CALEB: I brought a case of seltzer for this weekend. When we go to my in-laws', I'll alternate seltzers or colas with beer, and by the end of the night I drive home. Terry wouldn't let me drive if she didn't trust me, and she doesn't have as many opportunities to drink, so I'm usually the designated driver. However, I'm not sure why a buzz is pleasant, if it really is, or if I'm just escaping something.

DAVID: You maintain.

CALEB: It's the end of our four-day vacation.

DAVID: It could be a weekend thing, for you. Obviously, I'm doing this partly to get a "moment." It'd be a great ending.

CALEB: An "I know you but not as well as I thought I did" moment.

DAVID: Right. I can say, "You're an alcoholic." You can say, "Oh my god, what a pain-in-the-assperger."

○

CALEB: How about Laurie with drink?

DAVID: She has two or, at the most, three glasses of wine a night. She's a moderate drinker. She has it nicely under control. During the week do you drink?

CALEB: We drink less.

DAVID: What difference does it make?

CALEB: When I cut down on drinking, I lose weight. I've tried to gauge whether I'm a better writer when I drink. Is it conducive to thought?

DAVID: Uh—

CALEB: Alcoholics like to push their limits, but I don't like drinking beyond a certain point. Not that I'm in complete control.

DAVID: That's a good sign, that—

CALEB: The hangover should be avoided. All things being equal, alcohol tires you out and doesn't prolong life. The writer who lives longer and lives better produces more. I guess that's a reason to stop. I'm going to have to confront this sooner or later. So, last night, you drove into town.

DAVID: I wasn't comfortable with you driving.

CALEB: All right.

DAVID: Anyway . . .

CALEB: You're not off base.

○

DAVID: Milton Berle was at a Catholic charity event, had a glass of sherry, and they asked him, "Don't you want a second glass?" Everyone else was getting drunk. Berle said, "Jews don't drink. It interferes with our suffering."

Caleb laughs.

DAVID: That is to me *the* great Jewish joke. How does the other one go? The Catholic is thirsty and thinks he needs a drink, the Protestant is thirsty and thinks he needs a drink, the Jew is thirsty and thinks he's getting diabetes. . . . Umm . . .

CALEB: Needs a little work.

○

CALEB: Terry called to tell me about how Ava had a birthday party yesterday but neither of us—namely me—remembered to RSVP.

DAVID: Why couldn't she wait?

CALEB: She does this a lot.

DAVID: She's trying to make you feel guilty.

CALEB: If I leave in the morning and the refrigerator door hasn't been shut, she'll call me. "Caleb, you forgot to close the refrigerator door. Don't worry—I closed it—but I just wanted you to know." Or, "Why didn't you bring the dirty laundry downstairs?"

DAVID: It's an endless game of Tag—You're It or You Fucked Up. If I break a glass, it's a major tragedy. If Laurie does it, it's "Whoops."

CALEB: It's the bliss . . . ters of domestic life.

DAVID: Ouch. Not again.

○

CALEB: Let's see, would Khamta want me to leave the hot tub on or off? He probably told me and I forgot.

DAVID: Why would it matter?

CALEB: Waste energy or not? That's the question. I'll give him a call.

○

CALEB: (leaving message on Khamta's voice mail) . . . anyway, Khamta, give me a call.

DAVID: What are you going to do?

CALEB: I guess I'll turn the hot tub off.

○

On the road back to Seattle.

DAVID: The thing I liked best about Peter's novel [*A Young Man's Guide to Late Capitalism*]—what he was trying to get to (I think it's his big theme, actually, given that his father was a big muckamuck at the IMF)—is that if you view life as a chess game, you're going to miss it. Life, that is.

CALEB: Look at Bobby "Dear Mr. Osama" Fischer: the penultimate moronic genius.

DAVID: "Penultimate" means "next to ultimate," not "ultimate."

Caleb raises his eyebrows.

DAVID: Sorry. Chess game!

○

CALEB: Four Jews in the desert: three rabbis and one dissident rabbi. Or let's make it Caleb and his two friends versus David.

DAVID: Okay.

CALEB: Four Jews in the desert arguing over the Torah, and David Shields says to Caleb, "My interpretation of the Torah is right, and to prove it, I will ask for a sign." The blue sky clouds over, there's thunder, a few lightning bolts, and the skies part. David Shields says, "See, I'm right."

Caleb says, "That could have just been a coincidence, not a sign from God."

David says, "God, a little more help, please." Black clouds roll in, there's lightning all around, nearby trees are destroyed, a brief rainstorm, then the sky clears and there are a few puddles. David says, "Okay, admit it. I'm right."

Caleb consults with his friends; they come to a consensus: Caleb says, "That still could be a coincidence. Today could be one of those strange weather days."

David Shields gets on his knees and shouts, "God, I implore you!"

Clouds roll, part in the middle, a golden light floods the desert, and a deep voice booms, "David is riiiiiiightttt!!!!!"

David says, "What more proof do you need?"

Caleb and his two friends gather once again, and Caleb finally emerges and says, "Now it's three against two."

DAVID: Perfect. "I think you're totally wrong."

○

CALEB: A few words on post-childbirth belly: That belly is the home of our babies and that belly's beautiful.

DAVID: See, that's the thing: I couldn't say that without blushing if my life depended on it.

○

Pulled over on the side of the road outside Index, Caleb clicks off his phone.

CALEB: Well, I guess I was supposed to leave the hot tub on. I'll turn around. We're not going to be able to get you home in time for Natalie and Skype.

DAVID: Hmmm.

CALEB: Call Laurie, say that I fucked up.

DAVID: It wasn't any big mistake. You did what you thought you should. Unfortunately, Khamta called back.

CALEB: Fortunately. I mean, what if he called later? If I don't turn on the jets, the water will, little by little, turn green and nasty. The water needs to filter. He was cool about it.

DAVID: We'll get back around five?

CALEB: There'll be a little bit of weekend traffic around Sultan through Monroe. You might be late.

○

CALEB: We die, but I want to die old. I mean, if you die and you're forty-five and you have religion, you die thinking you will go to heaven and reunite with your loved ones. But I can't believe in something that I don't see as possible— that the afterlife is conditional on faith, that beyond being a good person you have to have "belief and swear allegiance to God," whatever that means, in order to enter heaven.

DAVID: There's always a rock in the garden. That rock is mortality or evil or both, but I really do love my life with Laurie and Natalie, my writing and teaching life. I have a blessed life and I hope it continues for another forty years.

CALEB: Then you won't outlive your father.

DAVID: Another forty-four years.

CALEB: If you're a religious moralist, you look for solutions within religion, but the secular or atheist moralist lacks absolutes. How do you tell people how to be happy when you can't define this for yourself?

DAVID: I'm not sure that being a moralist means you want everybody happy in the same way.

CALEB: Ever heard of Robert Ingersoll? Nineteenth-century atheist, way ahead of his time, loved his wife, a good father, a humanitarian, an abolitionist, a supporter of women's rights when these views were not in vogue. His speeches make for good reading. He said the most important question was, "How can you be happy?" And his answer was, "By making other people happy."

DAVID: Wrong question. Wrong answer.

CALEB: Right question. Right answer. First settle the question of yourself, then those around you.

○

CALEB: Money Creek Campground exit: the bridge and that tunnel are easy landmarks. We turn by that school bus sign.

DAVID: I'm gonna go in the house and steal a few crackers— or should I not do that?

CALEB: Khamta's mighty generous with his crackers. I don't think it would be a problem.

DAVID: I've still got an apple, grapes, cheese; you're welcome to any of my stuff, obviously. . . . What do you need to do?

CALEB: Go inside, get the key for the chain wrapped around the hot tub, open the hot tub, get the water circulating.

DAVID: Of all the things that could have gone wrong, this is obviously pretty minor.

CALEB: It's an extra hour.

DAVID: Maybe a little more. If at all possible, I'd love to avoid missing Natalie's call.

○

DAVID: You've traveled far more than I have, but when I've traveled, I pretty much find that worldwide there are seventeen types of people and you meet all seventeen types wherever you go, don't you think? It's not as if you arrive in Amsterdam or Seoul or Prague and suddenly realize: Oh my god, people are so different here!

CALEB: If you don't like your boss in the United States and every girl you go out with is a bitch, then overseas you'll hate your boss and your girlfriend will be a bitch.

DAVID: That's not what I'm saying.

CALEB: The dynamics of prejudice change, though. Koreans don't like the disabled or physical deformities.

DAVID: Meaning?

CALEB: There was this one teacher, American, who got fired because he was cross-eyed.

DAVID: They fired him for that?

CALEB: He couldn't control his pupils.

○

DAVID: Thanks for making such good time on the turnaround. Let me see if Laurie checked in.

CALEB: If no traffic problems, we'll be home in an hour.

DAVID: What town now?

CALEB: We're about to hit Gold Bar.

DAVID: All these funny names: Gold Bar, Index, Startup, Baring, Climax.

CALEB: Delivery needs work.

○

CALEB: You ever see *The Sunset Limited*?

DAVID: That Cormac McCarthy play with Samuel L. Jackson and Tommy Lee Jones?

CALEB: Jackson saves Jones from committing suicide, and they talk it out. Jackson's a no-luck ex-con and Jones is a professor, but no matter how Jackson tries to convince Jones that life has meaning, Jones holds on to the emptiness of life. There's a scene where Jackson recounts a prison fight and uses "nigger." Not "nigga," but "nigger." And Jones gets offended!

DAVID: Right. "Life has no meaning, I want to kill myself, but I'm going to be offended by the word 'nigger.' "

CALEB: What do you think of Cormac McCarthy?

DAVID: To me, he seems to be a complex and nihilistic version of *The Tao of Pooh*. His writing, from what I can tell, assumes the reader has never before confronted existential matters.

○

DAVID: Your ESL teacher's guide was published by a real publisher?

CALEB: Yes. We're talking triple-digit advance, and when you add royalties, I made well into four figures.

DAVID: You have three books. Two self-published?

CALEB: Technically, my sister published *Chinoku*. She publishes music and game books. She paid to have it formatted and so on. It's a puzzle book, more of a toy or game. It doesn't count for much.

DAVID: What are the three titles?

CALEB: *Chinoku, This Seething Ocean*, and *The World is a Class*. My publisher spelled "is" with a lowercase "i."

DAVID: What do you mean? Did you just not correct it?

CALEB: I didn't catch the error. I read galleys. She sent me a proof. I must have seen it a dozen times. *The World is a Class*.

DAVID: It's funny how your mind can fool you.

○

CALEB: Have enough Caleb for one weekend? Normally, friendship is marked by long periods of silences interrupted by selective extroversion, but I felt like silence wasted time and opportunity.

DAVID: I know what you mean.

CALEB: Every time I thought of something, I had to mention it. Earlier you said, "Caleb, we have to get to the point, not waste time, be succinct." But how can we do that? Conversation is a rough draft.

DAVID: That's where editing will come in. We'll cut from live moment to live moment, getting rid of the dross. Argue, asterisk, argue, asterisk, argue.

We need to make sure we go at each other. Life against art. I do think we embody those two antipodes. Not that I'm not interested in life or that you're not interested in art, but we need to ferociously defend how we have lived our lives. I have to say, "It's okay that I've never changed a tire, isn't it?" Or I say, "It's amazing that you speak all these languages and have traveled so extensively, but at age forty-three you're not yet the writer you want to become." Sound good?

CALEB: No. It doesn't sound good.

DAVID: Okay, then. If I'm being totally honest, I must admit I find it sort of depressing how much you've driven the conversation.

CALEB: That's not true.

DAVID: You have more stories. You're a better storyteller.

I'm out of stories, out of new ideas. I need to change my life.

CALEB: That's taken straight from that Rilke poem. Even your big heartfelt revelations are borrowed from books!

DAVID: It was an allusion, and you—

CALEB: Also, I don't want to fictionalize anything.

DAVID: What?

CALEB: What we say goes. I mean, yeah, add on a thought to a conversation—fine. Or if I paraphrase a quote and when I transcribe, I look up the exact quote, that's okay, that's in the spirit. Or if we talk about something on the second day, but it makes sense to bump it to the first day, I'm down with that. But I don't want to fictionalize some conversation with two bicyclists we never met. It didn't happen. I don't want to cross that line.

DAVID: Fine, but I can—

CALEB: If it didn't happen, I don't want to say it happened.

DAVID: I do.

○

CALEB: How often do you have life talks with Natalie? Who told her about the birds and the bees?

DAVID: In school, when she was twelve, they had to watch a movie called *Boys Like Breasts*. Basically, "You're about to get your breasts, and boys like them, so don't worry about it," that sort of stuff. We've had relatively few such talks with her.

CALEB: You talk about abstinence, condoms?

DAVID: She struggles with her weight due to the insulin issue and so—

CALEB: How's her esteem?

DAVID: That's a good question. She's a mixture of tremendous self-possession and deep insecurity (unlike the rest of us). The weight thing is a major problem for her. It's heartbreaking. She's beautiful.

CALEB: Life can be cruel. Kids can be cruel.

DAVID: Alert the media.

CALEB: Has she been asked to prom or homecoming?

DAVID: A bunch of people went together as friends. People like her, she has a lot of friends, and boys like her.

CALEB: Does she get any counseling for—

DAVID: She's seen so many doctors and nutritionists and specialists. She's been on so many medicines. We so hope she can break the cycle with diet, exercise, and meds. She's having good success of late.

○

CALEB: Have you ever been to counseling?

DAVID: Here and there. Nothing serious.

CALEB: What made you go?

DAVID: I saw speech therapists on and off until my early thirties. When I was trying to decide whether I wanted to be a father, I saw one psychologist a few times. He was pretty bad. He just kept saying, "What else are you gonna do?" Have you ever talked to someone?

CALEB: When I had my accident. I had serious bruising in the brain—in a coma for four days. Then I had a seizure right after waking up from the coma. My mind wasn't ready, and then they took off my cast. They set the bones wrong. I had a bulge in my wrist, so they had to rebreak it, set it with metal screws, and put it together again. I really took advantage of this and played the victim. But my head wasn't well.

I had the accident at the end of July and stayed at St. Luke's in Bellingham. I missed the first two weeks of senior year and was let out of the hospital in late September. My first week back, I had an episode at a football game. I had started at quarterback as a junior, and now I'm on the sideline with a back brace and a broken arm, telling everyone that I'll be ready to play in a couple of weeks. I'll get good real soon. The eyes of my former teammates and coaches were saying, "You've got a cast and shell around your chest, scars all over your face. Yeah, right."

A couple of my friends were going to the Oak Harbor High School dance afterward, and I wanted to go; the plan had been my mom would take us, wait outside, and then drive us home. But my mom wanted to take me straight home because I was acting nuts. I really wanted to go. It'd be my first dance in months, but she said, "No way—we're going home."

I became enraged, punched the door, opened it while she was driving, threatened to jump. My friends calmed me down. She dropped my friends off, took me home, and

I'm raving and angry, still. Then she called 911 and a policeman came to the house. Not an ambulance but a policeman.
I didn't know why. He came in and said that he just wanted
to take me to the hospital for a checkup and I'd come right
back, and I said, "Why? I'm fine. There's nothing wrong
with me." The policeman explained that I had to go, I'd
be examined, and if I was fine I'd come right home. So I
went in the back of the police car. My mom followed. My
dad stayed home with my sisters. They take me to Whidbey General, put me into a room, tell me that I'm not fine,
that I'm going to have to go back to St. Luke's for further
examination.

I exploded. I screamed, "Let me out!" I punched walls
until I was exhausted. They strapped me down, took me
in an ambulance to Bellingham. They said I bent the metal
plate in my wrist slightly. I remember going nutso toward
my mom, saying stuff like "Fuck you, you bitch. You
betrayed me, you bitch."

DAVID: What meds were you on?

CALEB: Dilantin. I'd already had the one seizure in August.
This time I blacked out, had another seizure, and woke up
strapped to a bed in the psych ward of the hospital. They
told me I'd gotten violent: they had to monitor me, and I
couldn't leave. I asked one of the nurses to take the straps
off. After a little bit they did, and I just started asking questions. I was completely normal, or so I believed. As if I woke
up normal, and now I was in this mental ward.

There were other patients—men and women, and they
all hung out in a common area, playing games or watching
TV. I played chess with a Vietnam vet, and I made a few

friends, if you want to call them friends. We each had our own room. I stayed there for two weeks.

I asked one older woman why she was there. She had outbursts/breakdowns, and she was maybe fifty. She was beginning to go bald, a little overweight, had gray hair and enormous breasts, and when I asked her when she was going to go, she said, "Whenever I want. I'm a voluntary patient."

I couldn't believe it. She volunteered? I asked her why. She didn't want to go into it but said that she sometimes felt like killing herself. So I went to the nurse, a guy with a beard, and asked about this. He told me I was also a voluntary patient. So I said, "I'd like to go." I didn't know that my parents had admitted me as a voluntary patient.

DAVID: "Guess what? You've been volunteered."

CALEB: I got angry. It wasn't a psychotic rage, though—more like I was rationally annoyed. I just tried to tell them I was fine, and this was ridiculous.

DAVID: I wonder if the meds wore off, or what caused the outburst.

CALEB: I'm not sure. I remember the hospital stay vividly. The Vietnam vet had been a Navy SEAL. He and I would play chess, and he had a very beautiful wife and daughter; the daughter was my age, too. I wanted to hear Vietnam stories, which he definitely didn't want to talk about. I told him he seemed normal, and he said, "Not on the inside."

The woman who was suicidal and going bald—she lost it once, just yelled and talked about killing herself, and the bearded nurse had to gorilla-hug her and calm her down. Her smock had slipped off and her breasts were showing, she was slobbering and drooling, and there were seven or eight patients watching.

My parents and friends visited, and I could take supervised walks—sometimes with this very kind nurse I had a crush on. She was maybe thirty. Very beautiful and calming. We'd take walks and converse, and I'd say how I didn't belong there, and she'd explain how they had to make sure. By now it's October—been over two months since the accident.

The last week or so I just played chess or card games and watched a little TV and read books, and waited, and gave up trying to argue, and that's how they knew I was sane. They knew I was sane because I no longer struggled; I accepted the situation.

DAVID: Part of it must have been that you saw yourself surrounded by truly crazy people.

CALEB: I couldn't make comparisons to McMurphy/Nicholson because I hadn't yet seen *One Flew Over the Cuckoo's Nest*, but when I saw the movie I knew I'd been there—at least a slice. I'd thought about killing myself in a not completely serious way. Maybe I'm in denial, even now. I imagined it.

After they released me I had to see a counselor in Coupeville once a week, and occasionally I'd go back to St. Luke's. My parents had to agree that I'd be kept under counseling. And I had to take all these personality tests before I could take a full course load at high school.

DAVID: What's that famous test, the Minnesota Multiphasic?

CALEB: Could have been. These questions were all over: Have you ever had a homosexual fantasy? Have you ever thought of killing yourself? Have you ever wanted to kill your mother? Have you ever wanted to sleep with your sister? When they finished, they told me I was in denial, according to "expert" evaluation. The only denial might have been about killing myself. I debated that one. I could imagine what it might be like to murder someone, but that's not the same as being murderous. I had a writer's imagination before I started writing, is how I look at it.

I'd taken these same tests in early September—same answers, and the psychiatrists had let me return to school; they hadn't seen my "denial." After the second test, the head counselor talked to me for a grand total of fifteen minutes and said, "Oh, I've looked at your results." She had practically no interaction with me and came up with this "expert" analysis. When I'd been truly insane, they let me out. When I was sane, they said I needed more counseling.

The school counselor and principal met, looked over these results from the hospital, and disregarded them. They put me back on a full course load. My parents stopped the counseling, but my depression was real. I mean, having broken bones and scars and not being able to play sports is depressing. It's not mental disease. You lose your wife or children or parents, something much more serious than what I went through, and you'll be depressed.

About four years after the accident I asked out a Coupeville girl, Michelle, I always thought was cute. In high school I wore heavy-metal clothes and had a mustache; she never paid attention to me. But in college I picked up a little fashion sense, and over summer vacation we were at a party on Whidbey Island, and she said something flattering about me in front of other people, so I asked her out. She accepted, we went out, she seemed awkward all night, I tried to kiss her, and she gave me a peck and left. Then I called, left a couple messages but never talked to her, and after a few days Brenda, a mutual friend, called to tell me Michelle wasn't interested. I'm twenty. It's not seventh grade.

I asked Brenda why, and she told me that Michelle thought I was odd. Brenda said that Michelle said, "I don't feel comfortable; he's weird." Brenda said, "That's just Caleb. Since the accident he's changed." And then Michelle said, "Caleb was off before the accident."

David laughs.

Thus my interest in the *DSM* [*Diagnostic and Statistical Manual of Mental Disorders*], leading to stuff like the *Rape Crisis Intervention Handbook*. Doctors try to evaluate rapists based on science. The conclusion always is, "This guy's going to rape again, and he'll be let out someday." I diverge. My point is I realized how important it is to appear sane. In *Speedboat*, Renata Adler says, "Sanity is the most profound moral option of our time."

DAVID: Don't I know it.

CALEB: Therefore, for the immoral, the criminal, it's to their benefit to appear insane. Any quasi-sane sociopath just needs to read the *DSM* in order to work the system.

DAVID: Do you see the world through the lens of the *DSM*?

CALEB: So you're familiar with the *DSM*?

DAVID: I practically wrote the fuckin' thing.

CALEB: It's riddled with uncertainty. A careful reading should make any doctor even more agnostic. I don't understand how any psychiatrist can testify at a trial as an expert. Rape and recidivism correlate—why do we need a psychiatrist to tell a judge that this or that rapist may or may not be a risk to reoffend? "This offender has a less than fifty percent chance of reoffending, so let's set him free." Why should society worry about violent recidivists? If you've committed a violent rape, not to mention murder, you never get set free. The end.

○

CALEB: Sometimes Terry suggests marriage counseling.

DAVID: When you guys are going through a rough patch?

CALEB: It's tongue-in-cheek. We watch *Curb* and Larry is getting counseling, and she'll say, "Doesn't that look like fun? Do you think marriage counseling could settle our differences?" I'll say, "You want to pay someone $150 an hour to tell him how you wish I vacuumed more often, and if I did you'd be in the mood more often?" The sex-for-chores carrot is a turnoff. Whenever she pulls that, I tell her I'll fuck her more often if she lets me drink more beer.

DAVID: You guys seem to get along pretty well.

CALEB: We rarely have arguments, although we disagree about everything.

DAVID: Same.

○

DAVID: I'm interested in how you had this brief flirtation with imbalance and how, from then on, you resolved to become a highly rational person. You decided you weren't going to go back there anymore.

CALEB: It made me an artist.

DAVID: That's a pretty fancy thing to say.

CALEB: My senior year, after the wreck, I was very introverted with occasional outbursts. It was when I "discovered" nature. I took walks or drives on Whidbey Island by myself, and I looked at myself, from the outside, for the first time.

There was a girl, Cathy, who I had kissed a couple days before my accident. I thought about her continually in the hospital, and she seemed glad for my recovery. We went out. My cast had been removed, I had a back brace, the bones in my right forearm bulged grotesquely; the surgery to reset hadn't happened. I wanted her to touch the bone. My arm is an orange-and-purple-and-blue deformed mess. She's trembling. Later I tried to kiss her. She gave me vomit face.

I get through my senior year. For the first time in my life I became contemplative. I started examining Christianity and went from drugs and alcohol to periods of abstinence followed by more periods of experimentation.

DAVID: But why do you think it turned you toward writing per se?

CALEB: Mark and Vince were the only two I could talk to about these things; each of them had a parent who had died. But some thoughts I wanted for myself, and I had these thoughts and needed to write. I started writing poems my senior year but didn't consider myself a "poet"—just writing thoughts and notes down on a piece of paper. Writing led me to philosophy and the Bible, and literature was the next step.

DAVID: I suppose it's pretty obvious how the stutter drove me inward as a survival mechanism. So, too, for you, this accident, though in a different way. "How did you go bankrupt?" "Two ways. Gradually, then suddenly." You went for suddenly. I went for gradually.

CALEB: I'm not bankrupt.

DAVID: Neither am I.

Both laugh.

CALEB: I wasn't a typical jock: I'd missed football and part of basketball. I scored high on the SAT, I graduated third in my class, and I got this army scholar-athlete award that they give to only a thousand people in the nation.

DAVID: Did you have to be from a military family?

CALEB: No. An army officer spoke at our high school assembly, mentioned various achievements, I was zoning out, and then he announced my name. I shook the guy's hand wearing a Judas Priest T-shirt, a mustache, and a quasi mullet. I finally realized how dumb the mustache looked and shaved it off before starting college. I met you two years later.

DAVID: I'm not sure how to articulate this exactly, but I forget that if a teacher comes along at the right time, that person can have a dramatic effect on a student's trajectory.

CALEB: Fishing for compliments?

DAVID: Trying to get us an ending.

CALEB: Your class humbled me.

DAVID: How so?

CALEB: You pooh-poohed everything I wrote.

DAVID: *(laughing)* I don't remember that. Didn't I criticize everybody's work?

CALEB: Of course, but you gave me a 3.0.

DAVID: Was that lower than usual?

CALEB: For a writing class where all you have to do is show up and participate, yeah. It was a wakeup. When that UW reporter asked me my main impression of your class, I told her I improved as a writer directly from your influence.

DAVID: Thanks. Hearing that is one of the rewards of teaching.

CALEB: My teenage students in Argentina gave me a parting gift and wrote, "Thanks for not only teaching us English but also for becoming our friend."

○

CALEB: We're home. This is 95th.

DAVID: Right. Is this your house? Well, that was painless.

CALEB: Tracy's car is here, too. Come on in.

DAVID: I can't. I'm already late. I'm supposed to be skyping with Natalie.

CALEB: Five minutes. I'll set the timer and kick you out.

DAVID: I can't. If not for the hot tub snafu, no problem—I'd love to—but, you know, I'm really trying to be present as a father and a husband.

CALEB: Meet Tracy. Talk a little bit with Terry. I'll try to think of something off-color to get a conversation going. C'mon, for our book.

DAVID: It's already past five. It'll take me another fifteen minutes to get home.

CALEB: Oh, this is excellent. This is the flip.

DAVID: Ooh, I—

CALEB: What's it going to be? Life or art?

A NOTE ABOUT THE AUTHORS

David Shields is the *New York Times* best-selling author of sixteen books, including *Reality Hunger* (named one of the best books of the year by more than thirty publications), *The Thing About Life Is That One Day You'll Be Dead*, and *Black Planet* (National Book Critics Circle Award finalist). He lives with his wife and daughter in Seattle, where he is the Milliman Distinguished Writer-in-Residence at the University of Washington. His work has been translated into twenty languages.

Caleb Powell grew up in the Pacific Northwest, has played bass in a band, worked construction, and spent ten years teaching ESL and studying foreign languages on six continents. Now a stay-at-home father in Seattle, he has published stories and essays in *descant*, *Post Road*, and *ZYZZYVA*.

A NOTE ON THE TYPE

The text of this book was composed in Palatino, a typeface designed in 1952 by the noted German typographer Hermann Zapf (b. 1918). Named after Giovanni Battista Palatino, a writing master of Renaissance Italy, Palatino was the first of Zapf's typefaces to be introduced in America. Like all Zapf-designed typefaces, Palatino is beautifully balanced and exceedingly readable.

COMPOSED BY NORTH MARKET STREET GRAPHICS, LANCASTER, PENNSYLVANIA

PRINTED AND BOUND BY BERRYVILLE GRAPHICS, BERRYVILLE, VIRGINIA

DESIGNED BY IRIS WEINSTEIN